INDOOR PLANT CARE 101

THE BEGINNER'S GUIDE TO HAPPY & HEALTHY HOUSEPLANTS

MICHE FERRET

CONTENTS

HEY PLANT LOVERS!

Make sure to not miss out on a free gift for you!
Free eBook Plant Journal made especially for you!
Just scan the QR scan code below or click this link!

Also, I have a Facebook community for houseplant
lovers just like you!
Scan the QR code or click this link to join!
Can't wait to see you there

To my husband Alex and my two sweet boys Alejandro and Axel.

With family everything is possible.

INTRODUCTION

"Plants give us oxygen for the lungs and for the soul."

— *TERRI GUILLEMETS*

Houseplants are the new 'IT' thing in the society we live in today, for reasons that should be obvious to most, but might be unknown to some. Aside from enhancing the atmosphere of a room, houseplants have the power to add a fresh feel to an empty or filled space that instantly lightens the mood of an overall room. Instantly, you feel a shift in your presence and that shift also affects your mental and physical well-being.

Are you still not convinced? Well, did you know that 15 minutes of interaction with houseplants can reduce stress within the body? Yeah, you heard correctly — it just takes 15 minutes of being in the same room as a plant. I'm sure most people would be overjoyed at the prospect of not having to take any sort of medication or melatonin pills to calm their body and allow it to rest. Research done by *Garden Pals* also found that houseplants increase productivity by 15% and remove up to 87% of airborne toxins in just 24 hours. So, in essence, you can combat your procrastination while simultaneously detoxing your environment without having to spend a dime. Incredible, right? This just goes to show that houseplants benefit you in more ways than one and getting one for your house would be a great investment.

With that being said, it is completely understandable that you may have one or two reservations about getting a houseplant of your own. Perhaps you might think you're not competent enough to handle what may seem like such a huge responsibility, which is understanding, of course. However, the reality is that most plant parents have killed at least one or two plants in their lifespan. Statistics even state that 70% of American homes claim to have at least one houseplant, and the average plant owner has destroyed at least seven houseplants in their lifetime. This may seem like a huge number, but it's a pretty average number in the grand scheme of things.

The reason why most people struggle to take care of their houseplants is because they lack knowledge of the basic information on how to keep their plants alive. Knowledge is power, especially in the plant kingdom, and having the right amount of knowledge will serve you in the long run. It's so important that you learn how to do things the right way as planting or taking care of plants isn't difficult at its core. It's also about a consistent routine and lots of intentional planning, which we'll be touching on in this book.

Everyone has been there before though, so don't worry if you don't get things right the first time around. Even some of the best gardeners in the market have had the same concerns regarding watering and sunlight exposure. The fear of leaving your houseplants alone while on vacation is a fear that many newbie plant owners share, but once you've read this book, you'll be void of any concerns when it comes to taking care of your plants.

So, take a deep breath and relax on your favorite couch while you unpack the goodness that is this book. I understand that there are, of course, different areas where you might find yourself in life right now, but, after reading this book, you will be a plant professional amongst your friend circle in record time! Everyone will be shocked by the things you'll know, but, more importantly, by how luscious your plants are.

Again, don't feel bad for killing a plant — we've all been there before. But, as long as you learn from your mistakes and understand what your plants need, you will be right on your way to becoming an expert when it comes to all things related to plants. In any case, that is most likely the reason you're reading this book in the first place. You want to be better — not just for yourself, but for your beautiful little houseplants.

One thing you should keep in mind is that being a plant parent is not a new phenomenon. Several affluent and well-known individuals are huge fans of planting, such as Oprah who is quite vocal about her love of plants on her Instagram. She often picks vegetables from her own garden that houses a variety of different plant life. Mark Ruffalo and Reese Witherspoon are also both huge fans of plants — the former is often seen engaging in all sorts of environmental activism, while the latter often has plants in each part of her house. These are just a few of the many celebrities that have made planting mainstream in our society.

Owning a plant is definitely a growing trend in our society. Whether it be including them in your social media presence or merely just having a strong affection towards plants, more and more people are becoming public plant lovers.

Gardening has changed the lives of countless individuals. In fact, *BuzzFeed* did an interview with their community where they asked for genuine reasons as to why their audience started gardening and the response to that one question was incredible. Recovering addicts opened up about how calming and therapeutic gardening was for their journey. For some individuals, gardening paved the way for families to be restored, despite a difference in opinions and general way of living life. And then, for others, plants represented the remembrance of a close relative that may have passed on.

So, naturally, I'm sure you may be wondering what makes this book different from the rest. Well, firstly, it took almost over a decade of personal experience with plants and dedicated research to finally craft this book designed specifically with you in mind. You're not just reading a book based on a theoretical point of view, but a book that has been tried and tested in the real world with real plants.

The question to ask however is what do plants mean to you? Why do you want to take care of your houseplant and what do your plants symbolize to you? Hold on to that thought and make sure to have your own personal reason as to why you care for your plants.

In the first chapter, we will be deep diving into why you would benefit from gardening and owning your own houseplants, so if it's your first time getting into gardening and plants, then this is the right book for you! Let's not waste any more of your precious time — grab your favorite snack and make yourself a hot cup of coffee as you move on to the first chapter.

BENEFITS OF HOUSEPLANTS

"A beautiful plant is like having a friend around the house."

— BETH DITTO

I magine you viewed your plant as a best friend or a constant companion within your home. Wouldn't you want to care for it with all your heart? Not only do plants offer company to those who live on their own or in a family, unlike a pet, but they also require little maintenance in order for them to flourish and live a full life.

In this chapter, we will expand your knowledge on the top seven benefits of having indoor houseplants, even if it's something you do as a mere hobby. Swanson's Nursery outlines seven specific benefits that houseplants have and some benefits may even come as a shock to some. Like, did you know that houseplants can increase your productivity and uplift your mood? RHS wrote a blog about how there are a myriad of psychological and physical health benefits that houseplants have, so ensuring you have a couple of plants within your space can allow you to obtain these benefits.

7 BENEFITS OF HOUSEPLANTS

1. It improves your mood

Yes — that's right. Houseplants are a proven mood-lifter, which may or may not come as a surprise to some of you. The calming and soothing effect of having plants in your home has the ability to boost happiness and improve your mood overall, which is a lot better than certain medications used to restore one's mood. An informative article by Hortibiz Daily detailed how having houseplants in your home, or even just in your vicinity, has the power to improve your mood within a short period. Houseplants give you a purpose for living as there is something other than yourself that you need to care for. Having plants in your room also improves the quality of your sleep, but make sure to choose the right plants, such as succulents, that release oxygen during the evening.

2. It reduces fatigue

Fatigue plagues our current generation that is driven by a non-stop work mentality. It is a serious condition which, according to Prestigious Plantscapes, presents itself in the body as exhaustion or depression. Often, those who are fatigued have a loss of appetite and are slightly more irritable.

Those who are fatigued tend to react a lot slower and lose their alertness, which can be quite dangerous in the workplace. There are various elements that can cause fatigue, from the lighting within the room to the number of hours which you work to the air quality of the building you are in.

So, I'm sure you're wondering — how do plants help reduce fatigue? Well, plants help to freshen up the air, lighten the room, and can even be used as a way to buffer noises, which are all great ways to reduce fatigue. You can also take your plants with you to work to help liven up your office space, which we will discuss in-depth in Chapter 8, where we describe the top succulents.

3. It lowers stress and anxiety

Marie Claire conducted some research as to how houseplants relieve stress. It was found that tension within the body was released by 40% merely through the implementation of plants in one's home. This is due to various factors, such as the color of leaves and teams, which are often green. Green, like blue, is a common and calming color. You may experience more stress relief if you use bigger plants, however, you must choose a plant that you know you can take care of well. Specifically, the Monstera, Devil's Ivy, and Dracaena plants are viewed as huge stress relievers and I have included these plants in the later chapters of the book, along with tips on how to grow them successfully.

4. It improves your focus and office performance

So, Desk Plants wrote an insightful blog about how plants affect your performance and overall focus and this was based mostly on research done at the University of Exeter. They noticed nearly a 50% jump in creativity and close to 40% increase in productivity just by the inclusion of plants in the office space.

Houseplants increase focus by firstly clearing toxins from the air and by providing psychological benefits, such as relaxation, upon viewing them.

5. It boosts your healing and pain tolerance

The American Study of Horticultural Science did a journal on how plants can boost your healing and pain tolerance. Have you noticed that in quite a number of hospital rooms, there are usually plants within the vicinity or outside the windows? This is not coincidental. It has been found in various studies that plants have a therapeutic influence. In terms of the ways it provides healing, a lot of patients are often forced to take an abundance of medications, so plants serve as a healthy distraction from the medication that is needed.

6. It improves the air quality

Did you know that plants are natural air purifiers? Well, they do this through a well-known process that most of you may have learned in school called photosynthesis. This is a process whereby plants take in carbon dioxide and toxins and release oxygen, which is the most important component of creating clean air. In fact, there are even certain plants that partake in the act of phytoremediation, which Plantera describes as "the process of any plant that has the ability to mitigate pollutants in the air, soil or water."

7. It eases dry skin and respiratory ailments

Plants aid in adding moisture to the air, according to Refinery29, which serves as a great way to ease dry skin. They also help with alleviating dust and toxins in the air as a result of the aforementioned process of photosynthesis and phytoremediation, thus it further helps in alleviating respiratory ailments. The peace lily is a great example of a plant that moisturizes the air and helps with dry skin, whereas spider plants create more chlorophyll which means they release more oxygen.

Freerad Books wrote a short blog documenting the story of a woman named Adria who used houseplants as a way of healing. She struggled with anxiety and an amalgamation of life issues, and the presence of plants definitely uplifted her.

Growing plants is honestly a lot easier than you think and there are definitely lots of ways for you to implement plants in your life for your betterment.

2

TIPS ON CHOOSING AND BUYING
YOUR PLANTS

"Plants give us oxygen for the lungs and for the soul."

— *TERRI GUILLEMETS*

Now that you know some of the biggest eye-opening benefits of houseplants, let's talk about incorporating them into your home — and the first step is to choose your plants!

One of the best things about houseplants is the variety of choices they offer. From gorgeous flowering plants like the Hoya Carnosa, Poison Primrose, Peace Lily, and African Violet to useful houseplants with remarkable health benefits such as Aloe Vera, Spider Plant, and

Rosemary — nature's got something for everyone. You could even get some plants that act as natural air purifiers like the Snake Plant which can remove all sorts of toxins from the air and converts carbon dioxide into oxygen at night.

The point is, choosing what houseplants you'll have might be just the first step, but it's the most exciting one! Whether you're in it for the aesthetics or could genuinely use better air quality in your home, picking the right houseplants is key.

Aside from your likes and dislikes, your houseplant choices should be consistent with the weather conditions where you live. That's because no matter how much love and care you pour into a houseplant that's unsuitable for your climate, the success rate could be depressingly low.

In this chapter, we will outline some basic tips surrounding how to go about choosing and buying your plants, where to go, and how to find the best plant quality on the market. We'll be deep-diving into the process of selecting the plants, 12 tips on buying your plants, and 10 secrets to becoming the Houseplant Whisperer.

So, without further ado, let's get into it!

12 TIPS ON BUYING YOUR PLANTS

No matter what type of plants you like, there are important factors to consider when it comes to buying them. Just a little research and planning beforehand can set you up for a successful journey of becoming the houseplant connoisseur. So here are 12 tips on buying your plants — this is where it gets interesting!

1. Plan and Research Beforehand

First things first, you need to assess your situation. It's different for everyone — from space constraints to weather and lighting conditions, everything needs to be taken into account during your initial planning.

Let's have a deeper look at such factors.

- **Sunlight**

Your home's natural lighting environment is a key factor to look out for. After all, they're gonna be "houseplants" so it's all about how the conditions are inside your home. Do you get enough sun? Do some spots offer shade for more sensitive plants?

Different houseplants have varying levels of sunlight needs and sensitivity levels. Some need bright sunlight directly shining on them for up to 8 hours, while others can only handle sunlight indirectly. If you want a houseplant that can only thrive in shade, you need to have a few shady spots in the house to accommodate them.

Before you set out to the nursery, become fully aware of the type of light your home gets in different areas. The best thing you can do is take pictures of each room during different times of the day to document exactly what you're working with!

You might already have a few spots in mind where you plan on keeping your houseplants, so the pictures can give you valuable insight into the sun situation in those areas.

- **Space**

The size of your houseplants also depends on the amount of space you've got for them, and how many you plan on keeping there. Space constraints are common for people living in the city — especially in apartments. The floor space is already limited, so the only options that make more sense are small house-plants like the adorable Baby Toes or Snake Plant (among many others). Another way to save floor space is to go for hanging plants like Bird's Nest Fern.

INDOOR PLANT CARE 101 | 27

- **Time**

Ask yourself how much time you can allocate for this new hobby? With some houseplants, you can get away with little to no care apart from the daily watering, whereas others are higher maintenance. If you've got a busy schedule and tend to be forgetful with daily chores, you'd be better off with safer choices like drought-tolerant houseplants. As you develop a habit of looking after your green friends, you can always pick up more houseplants that match up to your higher level of commitment.

- **Soil**

What type of soil do you have around the house? Get some soil test kits at the nearest hardware store and find out if you're working with loam, clay, or sandy soil as that also plays a role in making the right choice of houseplants.

2. No Impulsive Buys

As we've already established, there's a lot of thought and responsibility behind choosing your houseplants. No matter how gorgeous a *Fantasy Venice* plant looks as you drive by your local nursery, it might not be ideal for your home's environment and soil. You might not even have enough time to take care of it.

So, it's important to deeply study a plant and its needs, and ask yourself if you'd be able to provide a suitable environment for it at home. No impulsive buys!

3. Read Plant Tags

It's important to pay attention to the labels when you go plant shopping. Each plant has a tag containing keynotes that tell you if the plant is suitable for your situation. The info typically includes the plant's maturity, height, hardiness zone, as well as its requirements for light, water, and spacing. It's everything you need to know to figure out if the houseplant is right for you — so don't ignore the label!

4. Look for Unhealthy Red Flags

Sadly, not all plant babies at your local nursery might be healthy. Sometimes, the storekeepers won't even let you know unless you know what to look out for. That's why it's important to be aware of these red flags that tell you whether a plant is unhealthy right from the get-go.

- **Weeds**

Examine the plant closely to make sure there aren't any visible weeds right at its rootball's top.

- **Pests**

See if you can find any holes or spots on the plant's leaves. If so, it means pests have been chewing away at the plant or it has some sort of disease. If there are speckling spots, there will probably be pests hidden away under the plant's leaves or stems.

- **Brown or Yellow Leaves**

Your brand new plant baby should have healthy-looking leaves! So if the edges look a bit brown, that's not a good sign. It has probably been under-watered, and while it can recover with proper care, that's just not a risk you should take with a new plant.

On the other hand, plants at the nursery can also sometimes be overwatered. See if you can find a yellowish hue on the leaves to see if that's the case. It could also mean that the plant needs fertilizer.

- **Root Bound Plants**

Plants that have spent a significant portion of their lives in a nursery container tend to develop circling roots, and that's not ideal for proper water and nutrient absorption. Make sure you check the plant's root system before buying it. The professional at your nursery can gently lift it from the container to let you have a close look at its root system.

The plant should not have

- Roots that are growing out of the pot's drainage hole, because that's a sign that the plant needs to be repotted.
- Roots bundled up in a thick mat at the bottom of the plant and around its sides (root-bound).

5. Buds > Blooms

Flowering plants, like the ones we've mentioned at the start of this chapter, are some of the most gorgeous-looking plants you can add to your home — there's no denying that. However, you should buy buds and allow them to grow into that flowering stage rather than buying them *all bloomed up*. Choosing buds over blooms allows you to enjoy your flowers for a longer time. It also makes your house planting experience a more exciting and rewarding journey as you see the fruits of your labor grow into breathtaking flowers!

6. Size Doesn't Matter (With Plants at Least!)

When it comes to plants, smaller plants could be a better choice in many ways. Not only are they suitable for apartments and city homes with space constraints, but they also grow quicker. Moreover, they cost less and are generally less stressful to handle — definitely an advisable choice for new hobbyists.

7. Prefer Plants From Local Gardeners

Ask your nursery professional whether a certain plant comes from local farms. Local plants have a better chance of survival in your home since the conditions will be similar to their natural environment.

8. See If The Nursery Offers Warranties

In some cases, plants can, unfortunately, die within weeks or months after planting them at home. To cover that, larger nurseries offer warranties to secure their buyers against that risk.

When you finally begin shopping, make sure you ask if the nursery offers these warranties (because some smaller ones don't!).

9. Talk to Professionals

If you have any questions about your local plants or in general, you can always consult a certified horticulturist or nursery professional. They're happy to help since they've got diverse knowledge and years of experience to help new buyers out. You can even get customized plant recommendations that fit your home's conditions well!

10. Buy at a Nursery That Has What Your Plant Needs

Not all nurseries are alike. Here are the 3 main types of places you can get your house plants:

- **Botanical Garden Plant Sale**

Have you ever noticed a plant sale set up around your neighborhood around springtime? It even hits in fall sometimes and offers a mix of rare and common plants.

- **Large-Chain Nursery**

Since these big nurseries benefit from economies of scale, they can offer much better prices to the consumer. They get new plants stocked in pretty frequently, and you can expect them to offer warranties too!

- **Local Nursery**

Local nurseries are the most accessible choice for buying your houseplants. There's one of them in almost every large neighborhood and offers a wide variety of local-grown plants. The professionals working over there are knowledgeable about all the plants on display and they're generally super helpful.

11. Don't Visit the Nursery at Peak Hours

Here's another pro-tip, don't visit your local nursery at peak hours. You want to be there when very few customers are around to get easier access to the sales-people working there. As a new entrant to the world of houseplants, you'll have a lot of questions — and right-fully so! So, make sure you buy your plants during off-peak hours like night, noon, and even weekdays for a stress-free shopping experience.

12. Beware of Plants on Sale

Most nurseries have a selection of plants on sale for a slashed price. While they look appealing, you should give them a close look before purchasing them. Sometimes, you end up losing money on on-sale plants instead of saving it. That's because they could be root bound, drought-stressed, pest-infected, or have one or more diseases. After all, there's a reason why they're on sale!

10 SECRETS TO BECOME THE HOUSEPLANT WHISPERER

Now that you know how to select and buy your plants, let's look at the 10 secrets that turn you into *The Houseplant Whisperer!* Essentially, these will sum up the key points you need to know to successfully look after and grow plants at home.

The biggest fear of any new houseplant owner is to see their plants die due to their mistakes. The internet is filled with advice on how to keep your plants strong and healthy, but that much information can easily overwhelm someone who's new to the realm of houseplants. Thankfully, looking after your plants is no rocket science as long as you know and implement a few critical tips in mind — here they are!

1. Use the Correct Soil

Soil enables your house plants to nurture, grow, and sustain their stability. Different plant types thrive in distinct soil types — for instance, cactuses need less moist soil while orchids and ferns need maximum moisture in their soil. So, research and ask professionals to understand the soil needs of your particular plants!

Recommendation: Fast-Drying Soil

Here's a pro-tip: get fast-drying soil. No soil is suitable for all types of plants, but fast-drying soil generally works well with most of them! Since the soil dries up quicker, the plants get time to breathe even in between regular waterings. But remember to consult an expert before buying or changing up your soil as some types may or may not work with your specific plants.

2. Don't Kill Em' With Kindness (Overwatering)

Too much of anything is bad, even water! One of the most common mistakes that new (and even some experienced) plant owners make is overwatering their plants. No matter how carefully you choose your plants, how great your soil, container, and environment are for them — none of it can save them from the threat of over-watering.

Like soil, watering needs also vary between different plant types. You should be aware of how frequently your particular plants need to be watered. It mostly depends on your:

- Drainage
- Container size
- Plant size

Pro Tip: Use a Soil Meter

You might think your soil is dry by the looks of it and decide to give it some water — but that might be a mistake!

The visible part of the soil is its topmost layer, but looking at it isn't really a great way to tell if there's enough moisture. Instead, you should use a soil meter to check the moisture levels at its root ball since that's where the plant actually receives its water.

3. Smooth Drainage

A plant's root doesn't only absorb water, but also air! Without proper drainage, your root's air intake can be blocked out which not only hinders the plant's growth but also puts its life at risk. Using a container with excellent drainage is essential to keep your plant oxygenated. Ideally, you need to use an interior pot with a large drainage hole to let water pass through the plant smoothly.

4. Proper Lighting

If you remember the term "photosynthesis" from your school books, you'd know that plants make food out of 3 things: water, air, and sunlight. We've covered the first two so far, and the last one comes from proper lighting!

Since the plant will draw nourishment and energy from the sun, it needs sufficient exposure to natural light to grow and thrive in your home. But again, not every plant has the same tolerance and needs when it comes to sunlight. It can vary significantly between different plant types so make sure to look yours up online and talk to a professional to get expert advice.

The amount of light your plant gets needs to be just right. Too much or too little can both be serious risk factors, so here are some signs to look out for.

Signs of *Too Much* Light Exposure

- Plant colors lose vibrancy and seem dull
- A brownish hue on plants making them appear "sunburnt" or scorched
- Wilting leaves
- Brittle or dying leaves

Signs of *Insufficient* Light Exposure

- The plant's growth has seemingly stopped or slowed down
- New leaves remain small
- Yellowing leaves
- Thin growth
- No flowering or blooming

Pro Tip: Acclimate Plants with High Sun Tolerance

Acclimating means to let the plant get accustomed to a change in environment i.e. when you buy it from the nursery and bring it into your home.

Firstly, check if your plant has high sun tolerance. If so, place your new houseplants in the sunnier spots of your home to let them acclimate. After a month or so, move them to a neutral place for balanced sun exposure.

5. Repot When Needed

No plant thrives in an unsuitable pot. As soon as you see the following signs of your houseplant being unhappy with its current home, repot immediately.

- **The plant isn't growing**

Plants stop growing when they run out of space — and that's what happens when their container is too small. It causes root binding which slows down or puts a complete stop to their growth. Some people use this as a tactic intended to restrict their houseplants to a more manageable size.

- **You notice problems**

The plant needs repotting if there are issues with the container's drainage, the soil gets moldy or spotted, the leaves start dropping — or any other noticeable problems. This brings us to the next secret...

For in-depth guidance on how to propagate and repot your houseplants, read on to chapter 6.

6. Solve Problems (and Root Rot) Immediately

If you remember and implement all of the above 'secrets' with proper care, your plant's chances of getting root rot will be extremely low. However, houseplants are sensitive and it only takes a few mistimed mistakes for things to go wrong.

If and when you encounter root rot — the effects will start to show faster than you think! Within a week or so, you can use most or all of the gorgeous leaves and flowers that you (and the plant!) worked so hard for. It's a pretty demotivating sight to behold, especially for novice houseplant enthusiasts.

That's why it's essential to treat problems like root rot immediately at the first sign of ailment. Here's how:

- Repot and use fast-drying soil
- Use root rot treatment using supplements
- Continue to perform root rot treatment until the plant restores to full health
- Regularly treat the plant on a monthly basis to prevent future problems

7. Use (The Right) Fertilizer

Just like humans, plants need food to grow, and much of it comes from the soil. Out in the wild, the soil gets naturally replenished with nutrients from the dying and decomposing foliage. As you'd expect, this cycle of nature doesn't quite happen inside your home, which is why you'll need to use fertilizers to properly feed your houseplants properly.

Pro Tip: Use Liquid Fertilizer

There are plenty of fertilizers to choose from in the market. However, mixing some gentle liquid fertilizer into your watering container generally works great. It ensures a healthy supply of nutrients for your houseplants at regular intervals and doesn't even require the owner to remember and follow a feeding schedule.

8. Move It Around

Lopsided plant growth is one of the most common problems that new houseplant owners face. You could be giving your plant just the right amount of light, water, and fertilizer, but it can still grow lopsided if you don't move it around. That's because if you don't change its position from time to time, its sunlight exposure doesn't get distributed evenly across all sides.

Solution: To prevent lopsided growth and ensure even amounts of light exposure, make sure to slightly rotate your plant every time you water.

9. Cleaning Leaves

As mentioned at the start of this chapter, looking after your plants is no rocket science. Sometimes, it all boils down to something as simple as keeping their leaves clean! Keeping your plants free of debris and dust gives them a better chance to survive and grow.

That's because plants absorb air and light through their pores which can get clogged with dirt. Moreover, a layer of dust over the leaves also reduces the amount of light they absorb.

Both of these factors compromise the plant's ability to effectively perform photosynthesis. In simpler terms — clean your leaves, people! All it takes is a damp cloth or a quick rinse from a regular water hose. If you want to go the extra mile, you can use leaf sprays and lotion to get a glossy finish on top of your leaves.

10. Special Sundays

Specify one day of the week to give your plant some extra attention, care, and love. It doesn't have to be a Sunday, you can perform weekly checks on your houseplant on any day of the week. It'll help you notice small ailments and issues with your houseplants and take timely measures before they get worse.

You need to check for things like brown or dry leaves, root rot, pest, and soil status — including its moisture levels and drainage. While you're at it, say a few words of kindness to your plant because they're known to respond well to an owner's positive vibe! Little things like naming your plant and saying hello to them could go a long way.

That's all the secrets you need to know and apply to become the houseplant whisperer! Plants aren't high-maintenance at all — generally speaking. Just make sure to get the right type of soil, follow a consistent watering schedule (with some fertilizer in the can), keep an eye out for ailments, and take care of your houseplants' needs.

Speaking of needs, let's move on to chapter 3 which is all about a plant's essentials; soil, water, and light.

3

THE ESSENTIALS: SOIL, WATER, AND LIGHT

"There's something satisfying about getting your hands in the soil."

— *E.A. BUCCHIANERI*

I n this chapter, we'll look at the holy grail of plant life and growth — soil, water, and light. Plants need soil, water, a healthy amount of sunlight, and fresh air to synthesize foods through photosynthesis. While there's a lot you can learn about plant care, like intricate details on picking the right fertilizer or pest control, what *really* matters is getting your essentials right — the soil, water, and light.

So, let's look at each three of them in detail.

THE IDEAL SOIL FOR HOUSEPLANTS (AND WHY IT VARIES)

When it comes to selecting the soil for your house-plants, the approach isn't as simple as a one-size-fits-all solution. However, it's not too complex either! Generally, effective potting mixtures are fluffier and lighter than surface layer soil.

For instance, many vegetative plants prefer softer soil (which is why farmers plow the surface layer of soil in their land) but others naturally grow in hard rock crevices. So, depending upon the type of a houseplant's natural habitat, the ideal potting soil choice varies.

However, all houseplants invariably require these essential qualities in their soil:

- **Fertility**

The soil must have and provide enough nutrition to your houseplants for them to survive and flourish.

- **Water**

The soil should retain sufficient amounts of moisture to keep the plant nourished between regular waterings.

- **Anchoring**

The consistency of the soil should be firm enough to safely hold the plant's root system.

- **Air**

Roots need to breathe continuously so the soil should support enough gas exchange to let your plants live and grow.

The good news: A plant will survive in any medium or soil type that checks all four of the above boxes for it!

The not-so-good news: Not every soil mixture performs the same (or checks the above boxes in an equally effective way) for every plant, and that's where the overwhelming variety of soil mix options comes into play.

WHY WE DON'T RECOMMEND TOPSOIL

Topsoil comes with bugs, pathogens, and seeds. It's also too heavy for many houseplants which means you'd run the risk of suffocating them in a pot. Most houseplant deaths are caused by poor drainage and root rot, which means the "natural soil" outdoor isn't such a great idea.

POTTING SOIL 101 — TYPES

To give your houseplants the best fighting chance at life, you need to know their specific needs. Here are some common soil types you should know!

1. All-Purpose Potting Mix

All-purpose potting mix is one of the most commonly used soil mixes for houseplants. It's great at moisture retention and effective drainage, which helps fight the leading cause of houseplant deaths: drainage issues.

It's light and breathable, but still clumpy enough to provide a firm structure to the plant's root system. It's also pretty fertile — so yes, the "all-purpose" name makes sense!

2. Succulent Mix

This mix holds less moisture than its all-purpose counterpart, but that also means quicker drainage. It's typically more alkaline, has average fertility levels, and consists of sand and other loose components. It's also less structurally firm or clumpy than the all-purpose potting mix.

3. Epiphyte Mix

Did you know that high fertility in the soil isn't always a good thing depending on the houseplant you're working with? For instance, week-rooted epiphytes and orchids prefer soil that's slightly acidic, infertile, but structurally firmer and breathable. Epiphyte mix makes a perfect soil choice for such plants since it has exactly those properties and it's mostly made up of bark.

4. Specialized Mixes

By now, you hopefully understand that the soil needs of plants widely vary — which is why specialized mixes exist! These are essentially custom mixtures that are tailored to provide an optimized soil mix for plants with highly specific preferences. Examples include African violets, evergreens, azaleas, and many other complex plant species.

POTTING SOIL INGREDIENTS

Differences in soil mixes mainly arise from the supporting soilless ingredients they have. Some of these ingredients are great for additional structure, while others help add qualities like aeration, water retention, or additional fertility to the soil mix.

Here are a few ingredients that are commonly used in soil mixtures.

1. Soil Builders

✿ Sphagnum

Sphagnum is a natural plant material that's added to soil mixes as an ingredient for added water retention, aeration, and structural firmness. It's light and somewhat acidic (which some houseplants prefer, e.g. orchids).

Over time, the Spaghnum decays within the soil and offers a rich base of helpful microorganisms to aid the plant's growth.

Spaghnum comes in two states which both have unique uses:

Dried Spaghnum Moss: Dried Sphagnum Moss Consists of harvested and dried moss and comes with its gray, brown, or green fibers intact.

Peat Moss: Peat Moss is decayed Sphagnum sourced from natural peat bogs after a lengthy period of decomposition.

✿ Coconut Coir

Coconut Coir is another natural material that has gained lots of popularity as a valuable soil mix ingredient in recent years. Essentially consisting of coconut husk fibers, this material adds a ton of water-retention capabilities to a soil mixture.

It has higher water-retention tendencies than peat moss and it's also less acidic with a nearly neutral pH level. It doesn't have the same (or any) microbial value and fertility as decayed peat moss, but it's lighter and easier to work with. Moreover, coconut husk fibers are rich in potassium which helps improve a plant's calcium absorption. A lack of calcium in plants directly affects their growth, so a potassium-rich soil is a welcome bonus.

Pro Tip: Remember to wash coconut coir before use since it may come with salt from its natural environment. Simply place it in a bucket of water for about a week with a daily rinse and water change.

2. Drainage Materials and Aeration

The above ingredients are great for a boost in a soil mixture's structure and water absorbency, but that's not everything a plant needs. It also needs healthy aeration and drainage, and the following soil amendments are effective:

- Pumice
- Vermiculite
- Wood chips
- Calcined clay
- Charcoal
- Perlite
- Bark

Let's have a brief look at each of these.

✿ Pumice

Pumice looks like a spongy rock and naturally occurs as volcanic leftover. It's great for conditioning soil to improve its stability since it doesn't decompose or compact with time. While this neutral-pH ingredient doesn't add any nutritional value to the soil, its irregular pores improve water retention and provide adherence to useful nutrients.

✿ Vermiculite

Vermiculite is a process mica and it's one of the most water-absorbing soil ingredients out there. It's great for someone who tends to forget watering their plants regularly or just has super thirsty houseplants. It keeps the soil sufficiently wet between waterings and doesn't even decompose with time. It's lightweight, makes the soil breathable, and has a neutral pH level.

✿ Perlite

Perlite is essentially volcanic glass that has burst into tiny pieces from the extreme levels of volcanic heat. It's reusable, non-toxic, has a neutral pH, and occurs naturally.

It's highly effective at aerating your soil and also helps absorb some water (and fertilizer nutrients) through its micro-pores. However, perlite does slowly decompose with time. But since it's so lightweight, it tends to float to the top and jump out of the pot during watering so be careful!

✿ Sand

As we've established, no matter how fertile and nutritious your soil is, it still needs to aerate and drain well for your plants to thrive. That's where sand comes in. It's a great way to break up and loosen soil mixtures that are *too heavy* for certain houseplants. Using coarse grains of sand in your mixture can significantly improve drainage and aeration.

Tip: Don't go for small-grain sand if you're struggling with aeration since that can work against you!

✿ Wood Chips

Wood chips in soil mixtures are great at absorbing more water, keeping the soil moist, and provide little pockets for aeration. However, they use up the nitrogen in the soil and decompose pretty quickly. You can also go with pine wood chips instead of the regular ones for a reduced loss of soil nitrogen.

✿ Bark

Like many other ingredients in this list, bark is also an effective aerating agent when added to a soil mix, but it doesn't help with water absorption. In fact, bark's wax particles are hydrophobic and repel water to protect trees. It doesn't decompose as fast as regular wood, but does use up soil nitrogen and somewhat acidifies the soil as it decays.

✿ Charcoal

Charcoal is another popular soil ingredient as gardeners like to have it right at the bottom of their plant containers (or even mixed into the soil) to boost aeration and reduce odors. But if you're looking to buy it for all the pest-control and toxin-absorption tendencies that it's advertised to have, don't trust the ads so easily.

✿ Calcined Clay

Calcined clay is another strong soil mix ingredient as it boosts water absorbance and retention in the soil. It also improves your drainage! But don't let the water absorbency fool you into thinking that it'll turn into a clumped-up mess after watering because that's not the case. While calcined clay *does* comprise kitty litter, the variation that's used in soil mixture is processed at hotter temperatures to reduce the risk of sludgifying upon coming into contact with water!

3. Fertility Amendments

Up until this point, we've already covered some of the most important soil-related areas you need to consider when it comes to looking after your houseplants. In this section, let's look at the nutrients your houseplants need — the three main ones being potassium, nitrogen, and phosphorus.

Plants need lots and lots of these nutrients, and you'll find them labeled on almost all popular fertilizers. Generally, labeling includes an NKP ratio (chemical symbols for Nitrogen, Potassium, and Phosphorus respectively). Some come with a Nitrogen-rich formula in a 20-10-10, but fertilizers commonly strike a 10-10-10 balance between all three core nutrients.

However, that's not the only thing your plants need! They also need magnesium, calcium, and sulfur in smaller amounts – which is where other types of fertility amendments come into play.

- **Chemical Fertilizers**

Chemical fertilizers (also known as synthetic fertilizers) are one of the cheapest and most commonly used fertilizers for houseplants. They're water-soluble and can quickly deliver the recommended amounts of daily nutrition to your plants, though they're not as complete as organic alternatives.

However, a risk factor associated with them is their high concentration, making it more likely for novice planters to harm their plants by applying an inappropriate amount. That's why you need to balance out your formula carefully if you're making your own soil mix using synthetics.

- **Organic Amendments**

Organic fertilizers come from plants or animals, but they're not necessarily grown organically — there's no certification. Since they're not synthetically made, they're generally safer for houseplants. They can enrich your plants with the three major nutrients discussed above as well as the essential microbes and trace elements they need to grow and thrive.

However, this extra level of safety and added benefits come at a higher cost than synthetic alternatives.

- **Compost**

Another fertility amendment that's commonly used in domestic potting mixes is compost! The simplest way to understand composting is to see it as a natural recycling process! One plant decomposes and its nutritious remains feed your bright and youthful houseplants while also conditioning your soil mix with a fertility boost.

Compost can be store-bought or homemade — just make sure it's decomposed well!

- **Worm Castings**

Did you know that animal feces are known to be some of the best natural fertilizers out there? For instance, manure (more on this later) is one of the best ways to invigorate a dying piece of land for farmers! Going by the same principle, Vermicast (or, worm *poop*) makes for an incredible fertility amendment for potting soil mixtures.

It's an excellent source of balanced nutrition for plants and provides a variety of trace elements and microorganisms that houseplants need. Worm castings are readily available and they're odorless, safe to use, and easy to mix in any type of soil.

- **Leaf mold**

Lead mold that's well-decomposed and crumbly is another effective organic additive. It conditions the soil by enriching it with helpful bacteria.

- **Fish Emulsion**

In the realm of fertilizers, things that smell the worst most often work the best — and Fish Emulsion makes no exception. It's made from fish (hence the smell) and it's one of the quickest-acting soil amendments out there. It's an excellent source of nitrogen and soil microbes and completely safe to use — but it's pricey!

- **Manure**

Since worm poop works like a charm, it only makes sense that any type of animal feces would do the trick — right? Wrong! Manures from cows, horses, and chickens are high in urea and often too acidic to use safely in domestic potting mixtures. They can also have contaminants like seeds and herbicides.

However, composted and carefully aged manure is an exceptional tool to condition soil organically. But make sure that the type of manure you buy for your home use is safe and effective for the type of plants and soil you have. Do some research and consult an expert from your local nursery to make sure you get it right.

POTTING SOIL FOR INDOOR PLANTS — FACTORS TO CONSIDER

The safest bet is to go with a big brand name when you're in the market for potting soil, but that's also the most expensive route! If you go for cheaper alternatives, at least be choosy to make sure it doesn't cost you your plant's life in the long run.

Here are a few things to look for:

- Ideally, your potting mix shouldn't have topsoil.
- Since most commercial potting mixtures have synthetic fertilizers, it's important to check their NPK ratio and see if it's balanced.
- The potting mix should be fluffy and light to support lots of aeration. For these qualities, look for vermiculite, perlite, pine bark, and peat moss in the ingredients.
- If a soil mix has too much styrofoam or sand — that's a red flag. However, smaller amounts are okay.
- Some cheap potting mixes come from exhausted mulch or landfills, so beware of the soil containing wood chips, colored items, or roots.
- Some mixes come with gels or crystals that enhance water retention, but they're not as reliable as you may think. Sure, they'll cut down watering needs, but they don't last forever. Some plant owners rely on these shenanigans and go on small vacations only to find their plants withered and brown when they come back. For novices, these mixes will only complicate plant care by making watering cycles more confusing and uncertain.

- Don't rely too much on "slow-release" or "starter" soil additives. They'll add to the plant's nourishment at the beginning, but you don't know for how long. Soon, you'll have to use additional fertilizer, but there's no way to tell if your "slow-release" additives are gone just yet — which further complicates plant care for beginners.

MAKING POTTING SOIL FOR INDOOR PLANTS

To make the best possible potting mix for your house-plants, it's important to know what you're aiming for. Ideally, it should have excellent nutritional value, desirable top soil consistency, and suitable pH levels. Instead of reading the ingredients on a thousand different labels, you can always make your own potting mix — DIY style. This chapter has covered the basics comprehensively, and if you've read it all — you're ready to start experimenting!

Making your own soil mix requires way more effort than just picking something off a rack, but the exciting process is worth it as it's customized to your plant's needs. As a bonus, you'll be aware of exactly what your soil mix consists of!

There are many different potting mix recipes that work, but here's a simple formula you can follow.

Soil-Building Material (60%)

60% of your DIY potting mix should consist of soil-building material. Examples include coco coir or peat moss to achieve an absorbent and light structure.

Nutrients And Aeration Material (40%)

The rest of your potting mix components (40%) should be all about adding nutritional value and aeration to the soil.

Perlite is one of the best ingredients you can add to enhance drainage and get a massive boost in aeration. You can add fertilizers and aeration material in a 10-30 split, which means that your soil will have 30% of perlite and 10% nutritional supplements like synthetic fertilizers or worm castings.

With that said, there's no one-size-fits-all approach that'll perfectly apply to any houseplant in all conditions. Feel free to switch up the ratio and ingredients according to the specific needs of your plants. Again, the experts over at your local nursery will be happy to help you out!

WATER FOR HOUSEPLANTS

What's the first thing that comes to mind when you think about plant care? Water!

Many plant owners wonder if it's okay to use tap water for their houseplants. It generally is, unless your tap water is softened. That's because softened water has salts that can build up in your soil and become problematic in the long run.

Even chlorinated water doesn't harm most houseplants in any way, but a filtration system is still preferable to limit chemical exposure. Water also shouldn't be too hot or cold as both can damage your leaves.

Another great alternative is rainwater! It contains traces of nitrates that are essential for growth. So, you can get into the habit of collecting rainwater for your houseplants. As a bonus, stored rainwater can also encourage algae growth and attract insect larvae which means more organic matter for your houseplants to feed on!

Watering Amount

Different plants vary in their watering needs. Some need more than others, and if you don't know how much your houseplants require, you can get an idea from their respective natural habitats. For instance, houseplants that come from tropical origins (e.g. philodendrons) will generally have large leaves and absorb lots of water. On the other hand, desert cacti will thrive and do even better if the soil remains dry between waterings.

If you're noticing signs of slowed-down growth even though your plant hasn't reached its full size yet, it's advisable to reduce your watering amounts or frequency (or both) until you see an improvement.

Sometimes, houseplants grow faster or slower depending on the season and time of year. Many plants — especially the tropical ones — grow more in the summer and spring and tend to slow down in winter and fall.

Timings for Watering

Watering is a sensitive issue in plant care as many new owners regularly forget or delay it. On the other hand, overwatering could pose even more issues. So, if you're new to this houseplant life — it's important to make and follow a strict watering schedule for your plants.

However, not all plants need to be watered daily. For that, you should remember to check on them every couple of days to see if they need a drink. Signs like wilting leaves mean that your plant desperately needs water, but you shouldn't let them get to that point!

So, even if your plants look healthy, stick your finger about an inch into their soil and check for moisture. If there is none, water it up! If the soil feels damp down there, check back in a couple more days. You can also use planting assistant apps to give you prompt reminders.

Tip: The longer the water stays on leaves, the higher the risks of disease! That's why watering in the morning is better (instead of the evening) as the sun dries out residual moisture on leaves.

Watering Quantity

Most people underestimate the amount of care and thought that should go into watering houseplants. It's not as simple as dribbling in very little water whenever the soil looks dry. While you won't be overwatering your plants that way, it doesn't help the plant either. That's because the root isn't situated anywhere near the surface of the soil. Even if a tiny dribble of water wets up the surface, the water will probably not even reach the root.

Instead, you should continue pouring water until it starts to drain out of the pot hole(s). Some house planters also place a saucer under the pot since plants can soak up the drained water after some time. That's also a safe practice as long as you remember to empty it out in 10 minutes to prevent root rot.

You can also water your plants by filling up the saucer under them and let it get absorbed through the drainage holes. To prevent overwatering, you should stop filling it up when the plant ceases to absorb any more of it.

Are You Overwatering Your Houseplants?

Overwatering is one of the leading causes of plant deaths and problems. Plants can *literally* drown when there's too much water since roots cannot absorb sufficient oxygen in waterlogged soil.

That's exactly why your pots have drainage holes. But even they're not enough to save the plants from the risks of overwatering because soil that's constantly wet can also choke airflow. It's important to know a few key signs of overwatering to be able to take corrective measures before it's too late.

As discussed above, the biggest signs of overwatering are yellowing leaves and a noticeably slower or stunted growth.

The tricky part is knowing the difference between yellowing leaves and wilting, which point toward overwatering and underwatering respectively.

When in doubt about these symptoms, insert your fingers about an inch into the soil and check if there's moisture or dryness.

Adjust your watering quantity and frequency accordingly and see if the symptoms start to slowly fade away. If not, try tweaking their light exposure levels and temperatures and get them as close as possible to their natural environment.

Your nose is also an effective tool to check for overwatering issues. Since excess moisture leads to bacterial and fungal growth in soil, an overwatered plant will generally have a pungent smell. It gets even worse when root rot starts to develop.

On top of that, if you notice fungus gnats flying around the vicinity of your houseplants, you probably need to cut back on your watering.

Overwatering ultimately leads to plants' death, but it doesn't have to go that far. Even if you've overwatered for some time but detect the issue in time, the damage isn't irreversible. Simply give the plant some time to dry out its soil before the next watering session. From there, be more careful and follow the watering tips shared here.

Repotting your plant in fresh soil mix is also a great idea to give your plants a well-needed fresh start, but it might not be necessary in every case.

One thing's for sure, watering your plants appropriately is a skill that develops over time. You'll learn to get your watering quantity and frequency right the more experience you get as a houseplant parent. You won't make newbie mistakes like forgetting to water or not being able to spot obvious signs of overwatering.

Once you feel more confident in your watering habits, you can move on to plants that require a bit more care and attention.

NATURAL LIGHT SETTINGS — PRIMARY TYPES

As discussed in earlier chapters, different plants prefer varying levels of sun exposure needs. Here are some main types of natural light settings that you should know:

- **Low light or full shade**

Most people with no planting experience are unaware that some plants prefer shade or low light conditions with minimal sun exposure. While that's not true for most plants (like flowering ones), species like zz plants, cast iron plant, dragon tree, and the mother-in-laws thrive in lower light conditions.

Such houseplants are best placed at a north-facing window to limit their exposure to the sun as much as possible.

- **Full sun**

Most plants and trees need all the sun exposure they can get as it's an integral part of their photosynthesis. However, that's not the case for many house plant species. Many of them get damaged and might even fail to survive under too much sun. But succulents and desert cacti are some examples that always need to be in a sunny spot during the day.

Such species should be placed near a south-facing window to maximize their exposure to bright light.

- **Shade and partial sunlight**

Some plants prefer a moderate amount of both, light and shade. They're too sensitive to face the full-on light and heat of the summer sun at midday, but they still need a sufficient amount of bright light throughout the day to thrive and grow.

These plants should ideally sit near an east or west facing window to get balanced levels of shade and sun throughout the day.

- **Bright conditions without direct sun exposure**

There's another category of plants that prefer bright light but can't directly take on the sun for extended periods. Most foliage plants have such lighting needs and should be placed a few feet away from a south-facing window. In that position, they'll still be exposed to bright daylight from the window, but it won't be shining on them directly from the sun.

Identifying Problems

Just like there are noticeable signs in plants to point out watering issues, a plant will also tell you if it's getting too little or too much sunlight. For that, you'll need to know and look out for these signs:

✿ **Too Little Sun**

- Slow, weak, or no growth
- Newer leaves remain small
- Yellowing leaves
- Flowers not blooming (in flowering plants)
- Falling leaves

❁ Too Much Sun

- Leaf color fades
- Drooping leaves
- Shriveling leaves
- Shriveling flowers
- Dying leaves and flowers

Artificial Lighting

While natural light is the primary ingredient of plant food for most species, some house plants may need artificial lighting to thrive in an indoor environment. That's especially true in the winter when it's pretty light-less throughout the day. If your plants get no more than 7 hours of daylight, that's when artificial lighting generally needs to make up for it (especially for more light-hungry plants like flowering species or succulents).

Artificial lighting helps keep plants looking healthy and green even when they don't get sufficient natural light exposure. They can also help keep flowering plants in bloom (such as the African violet) when they're desperate for daylight in the winter months.

Household Lighting Is Not Suitable!

You might think artificial lighting means regular household lighting, but that's not the case. Your best bet would be fluorescent lights. You can use any variation of them that's easily accessible (or affordable), including fluorescent lamps which you might have lying around the house already.

There are many different fluorescent lighting options that are specifically designed for indoor plant care. Gro-lux fluorescent bulbs are a great example that offers a special mix of red and bright light spectrums for optimized artificial lighting for indoor plant growth.

KEY TAKEAWAYS

This chapter has deeply covered three of the most important elements of plant growth — soil, water, and light. If you want to see your houseplants grow and thrive, you need to get all three of these right!

But, every plant parent makes mistakes, and the best part is that most of them are rectifiable if you spot the relevant signs in time. We've shared them too, as well as what you need to do to reverse the damage. Be sure to revisit this chapter regularly to know your do's, don't, and signs to look out for to ensure optimal soil, water, and lighting conditions for your houseplants.

4

NATURAL ALTERNATIVE
PESTICIDES

"Plants do not speak, but their silence is alive with change."

— *MAY SARTON*

In this chapter, we're going to talk about how you can protect your little green beans from those pesky intruders that get in the way of their good health, survival, and growth. We'll cover ways to identify some of the houseplant pests and why you should try to use natural pesticides. I'll also share my 7 favorite recipes for homemade plant sprays, as well as a few effective measures to prevent any future infestations.

Too many plants die to thrips and different types of pests, and it's one of the most baffling problems for novices to deal with. I myself have experienced it first-hand in my earlier days of plant care.

Only a few weeks into bringing in a new batch of houseplants — having carefully optimized everything from their soil composition to their positioning for light as well as precise watering sessions — I started noticing silver-ish discoloration on the leaves of my African Blue Basil (a relatively rare houseplant). I didn't even know what it was, how it happened, and how to treat it.

Like any other newbie, I didn't think too much of it and tried being more careful with my watering. Little did I know, it was a thrip infestation causing it.

It only took them only a month or so to ruin the whole plant. It was so gradual that by the time I started to take the problem seriously, it was already too late and I had to get rid of it to protect the other plants in my yard.

It was painful, but thankfully (and hopefully), you wouldn't have to go through any of it. As long as you read and implement all of the detective, preventive, and corrective information shared in this chapter, your plants should be safe from pests.

Had I known all this back then, I'd have gotten rid of the thrips in time — not my beloved African Blue Basil. But, at least it didn't die for nothing — you get to learn from my mistakes.

So, without further ado, let's get into it.

IDENTIFYING THE SEVEN COMMON HOUSEPLANT PESTS

This list of seven houseplant pests doesn't cover each pest type out there, but these are the most typical ones. These are the ones that bother an overwhelming majority of houseplant enthusiasts, and they'll most likely be the ones you'd be dealing with (hopefully not).

1. Common Brown Scale (Coccus Hesperidum)

If you ever wonder why your plant suddenly appears shinier than usual, you might be dealing with scale pests. They're so small that they're only visible upon closer inspection — that too, hidden away at the under-side of your leaves.

There are many types of scale pests, but the most common variety is the "Coccus Hesperidum L" — or the brown soft scale in *English*. They won't look like an insect at first glance (unless you're a planting pro). Often brownish in shade, they're as small as 3 to 4 millimeters in length and about 2 millimeters in width. Some of their other colors are amber, yellow, and similar shades.

They most often exist in the form of clumps along the stem of plants sucking away at it — so that's where you should look if you're checking for the common brown scale.

Scales can be a hassle to deal with because they're not too temperature-sensitive, which means they can survive all year round in most parts of the world. It also means they'll also be reproducing all day, all night. However, they are relatively immobile and don't spread around your entire indoor collection as fast as some of the other pests on this list.

2. Mealybugs (Pseudococcidae families)

Another extremely common species of pests are the mealybugs. They have a cotton-ish appearance, and also form clumps like the brown scale, but they are much more mobile. They can infest anything from succulents to potato plants. They're known for being an overnight problem and *"just show up"*.

Mealybugs are scaled insects, but they're unarmored (unlike the brown scale pests). Due to their spontaneous visits, they're also harder to control.

They're small, cottony, and soft. However, their white color is pretty apparent on plants. This means they've got a natural disadvantage at hiding, but that doesn't stop them from trying. They'll find the cleverest spots to hide to secure the best chance of survival. Common places include the inside of an unfurled leaf or the crotch of a houseplant.

One of their most problematic qualities is how fast they multiply. A single female mealybug can lay up to 600 eggs! They take about a week to start hatching and the sudden explosion is enough to baffle any houseplant owner — novice and pro alike.

Some effective ways to deal with mealybugs are:

- Summoning an army! By an army, I mean introducing two helpful insects to an infected plant. They're called the "Green Lacewing", and the "Cryptolaemus Montrouzieri" — also called the "mealybug destroyer" (literally). They'll work together to hunt down mealybugs and do all the hard work for you.
- You can also try spot treatment which involves dabbing isopropyl alcohol directly onto mealybug clumps using a Q-tip. This instantly kills them, but your Q-tip won't reach those tiny spots that the mealybug destroyers can

easily access. Therefore, a combination of both methods is by far the most effective way to deal with these pests.

3. Aphids (*Aphididae family*)

Here are the most popular unwanted guests in the houseplant world — Aphids. If you've only got tropical houseplants, you're pretty much safe from these pests, but not if you have any sort of food crops.

Their sole purpose in life is to pierce those juicy plants with their mouths and suck away at the gooey sap — which is essentially the lifeblood of your precious plants. They also excrete sweet and sticky honeydew from the rear end, which only worsens the pest situation as it attracts other ants and pests. The aphids themselves multiply like crazy, too. Basically, you don't want these anywhere near your houseplants.

They're green, soft, squishy, which makes sense since they're filled with plant juice. They're also oddly satisfying to squish between your fingers — mostly because it feels like sweet vengeance for sucking away at your babies!

They're generally wingless, but if you find wings on them — it means they're big enough to hop and fly to infest the other nearby plants.

The best way to deal with these is to spray the infected plant with water. Afterward, look closely for residual aphids and crush them. Repeat this cycle for a few days until things start to get visibly better. If it doesn't seem to work, you can introduce beneficial insects like the ladybird larvae and the green lacewing larvae.

4. Common whitefly (Trialeurodes vaporariorum)

At first glance, the common whitefly appears similar to white moths — but much smaller in size. They share many similarities with the Aphididae family, as white-flies also suck away plant juices and produce honeydew (which attracts more harmful ants, insects, and sooty mold).

A novice might even mistake them for mealybugs, especially since they also like to congregate on potatoes and potato plants. These little critters continuously suck away at your plants while also simultaneously laying eggs — some of the worst qualities a houseplant pest can have. What makes them even more annoying is their ability to alight on other nearby plants and spread like wildfire.

If left unchecked, a whitefly infestation can significantly weaken and eventually kill your houseplants.

Their weakness is that they're attracted to the color yellow (for whatever reason), so yellow sticky traps are your best countermeasure against them. As a last resort, you can also unleash beneficial insects on infected plants to deal with whiteflies. Examples include the ladybird beetle, the whitefly parasite, and the green lacewing.

5. Red spider mites (Tetranychus sp.)

Mites technically aren't insects, but they're still a class of houseplant pests belonging to the arthropod category (same as insects). But what matters is that they're some of the scariest pests you can find on your houseplants simply because they're stubborn and just won't go away (easily).

Spider mites are almost invisible to the naked eye. You'll need a magnifying glass to check for them.

[Warning: Don't take a magnifying glass to your plant in the sun as it can severely burn and damage the leaves]

You can also notice a reddish film building up across the leaves' bottom without a magnifying glass. If that's accompanied by webbing, it means you may have a red spider mites problem. Take a magnifying glass to the film to confirm if that's the case, and if so, you'd be looking at a ton of bright red tiny critters.

While they have an intimidating appearance, there are ways to deal with them. Firstly, make sure to always have the humidifier on inside the house (if the infected plants are situated indoors) as mites thrive in dry conditions. You should also keep the plant wet and its soil moist (without overwatering it). On top of these measures, consider introducing like the minute pirate bugs and the lacewing larvae as they're natural predators to spider mites.

6. Fungus gnats (Bradysia sp.)

Fungus gnats aren't technically classifiable as houseplant pests, but they're far from irrelevant to this discussion. They're not generally interested in your plants, but rather the fungi within the soil. This means they're not really harmful for the houseplants, but definitely annoy people — especially if the plants are indoors.

They look like fruit flies and like to buzz around soil, which is also where they lay eggs to multiply. While the adults are harmless, their offspring — not so much. You can handle these "pests" with some BTI from your local nursery, sprinkling it over your soil. For the adults, some yellow traps often do the trick.

Like the other pests on this list, fungus gnats also have natural predators like the Stratiolaelaps Scimitus (a type of mite). So, if the BTI and traps don't show results in about 3 days, consider introducing these little soldiers!

7. Thrips (Order: Thysanoptera)

Thrips, the nemesis we talked about at the start of this chapter, the murderers of my African Blue Basil! Gone, but not forgotten.

Anyways, thrips aren't as common as some of the other insects on this list, but they're a nightmare for anyone who has had to deal with them. The worst part about them is how quickly they spread, and how difficult they are to get rid of. Thrips damage your plants by puncturing their outer layer, leading to a visible discoloration of the leaves making them appear silver-ish. The tiny bits of black frass (essentially insect poop) spread all over the infected plant's leaves are also an unwelcome side effect.

They're definitely hard to miss even if you give your plants a quick little glance every day. To the naked eye, they appear like long black specks with a pointy back-end. Looking closer with a magnifying glass, you'll see black and red or black and brown patterns extending throughout their long bodies, six legs, and two "antennas" on their head.

If you notice these symptoms, the best thing you can do is snip away and re-plant some healthy cuttings just in case you fail to treat and revive the affected bits. Then, your anti-thrip arsenal includes blue sticky traps (since they're attracted to the color blue) and introducing natural thrip-predators like the Minute Pirate Bugs (Orius Insidiosus) or the Neoseiulus Cucumeris (conveniently nicknamed "Thrip Predators").

And with that, we've covered the seven common types of houseplant pests that you need to know about. But, your greatest weapon against them is natural pesticides! Not only do they fight pest problems, but they're also eco-friendly and better for your soil quality in the long run (as compared to synthetic pesticides)!

BENEFITS OF USING NATURAL PESTICIDES

Let's discuss the benefits of using natural pesticides in depth.

1. More eco-friendly

Opting for natural pesticides over synthetic ones reduces the carbon footprint of your houseplant hobby. So, if "going green" matters to you (as it should), natural pesticides are the way to go.

2. Better long-term performance

Pests can develop a tolerance to synthetic fertilizers over a long enough period of time. That risk is much lower with natural pesticides, which means they perform better in the long run.

3. Safer and healthier

If you're buying pesticides for your home garden (with food crops in it), natural pesticides will also be a healthier choice. That's because your soil fertilizer has a direct impact on the fruits and vegetables that come out of that soil, and the fewer the chemicals, the safer the fresh produce will be for you and your family. Hence, natural pesticides are also a healthier choice.

4. Natural pesticides promote better soil quality

Natural pesticides are also better for your soil quality as compared to their synthetic counterparts. As we've learned so far, good soil leads to healthier plants and improved growth. It also means there are lower risks of contamination or other unwanted effects like slow or stunted growth.

7 HOMEMADE PLANT SPRAYS

So, synthetic (chemical-based) pesticides are bad for your plant, soil, and the environment — what should you do? Well, the easiest (and most cost-effective) alternative is to make your own natural pesticide plant sprays at home!

They're easy to make, and much safer than the products you'd buy at garden centers since they'll consist of 100% natural components. There's no gray area in the ingredients either since you'll know exactly what you've added to make your DIY pesticides. As far as their effectiveness is concerned, you'd be surprised how well they work at keeping insects and mites away!

Here are my 7 favorite homemade plant spray recipes.

[**Warning:** Make sure you test all store-bought or homemade solutions thoroughly before fully exposing your plants to them. This is because some sprays or pesticides (both, homemade and store-bought) can have adverse reactions with some plants and cause severe damage.]

1. Garlic Oil Spray

Garlic has a strong aroma that is strong enough to annoy humans at times, let alone tiny pests. Its scent works great as the main ingredient in a natural insecticide.

You'll need

- 1 garlic head
- 2 cups of water
- 2 tbsp of mineral oil (you can also use vegetable oil)
- 1 tbsp dish soap

Method

1. Peel and puree garlic cloves in water and oil, and let the mixture sit for 12-24 hours.
2. Strain it, add dish soap, and stir well.
3. Use a spray bottle to treat infected spots in your home garden.

It doesn't get much simpler than that, does it?

2. Soapy Water

Another effective homemade plant spray is soapy water. As the name suggests, it's even quicker and easier to make than garlic oil spray.

However, it isn't effective with all types of pests out there, but still helps control the following:

- Mites
- Aphids

- Japanese beetles
- Squash bugs
- Other small bugs
- Cabbage Moths
- Beetles

You'll need

- 1 tsp dish soap
- 1 tbsp vegetable oil
- 8 cups of water
- 2 tbsp baking soda

Method

Mix all ingredients together and pour it into a spray bottle.

Literally a 1-step procedure, and all you need is a spray or two on infected areas in your garden and it works well against the pests mentioned above.

3. Cayenne Pepper and Citrus Oil Spray

If you see fire ants and small ants lingering around your plants, this is the natural spray you need. The capsaicin in cayenne pepper keeps spider mites and many other types of insects away from your houseplants.

You'll need

- 10 drops of citrus oil
- 1 tsp powder cayenne pepper
- A cup of warm water

Method

Mix everything together in a bowl and transfer it carefully into a spray bottle. Be careful not to get any of it on your hands or eye as the capsaicin can burn and cause injury.

4. Salt Spray

One of the simplest ways to battle spider mite infestation in plants is to spray the affected area with salt water. Every household already has the required ingredients at home, so it's one of the most accessible homemade sprays on this list.

You'll need

- 16 cups of warm water (1 gallon)
- 2 tbsp salt (preferably Himalayan)

Method

Mix the two ingredients together and pour it in a spray bottle. Spray it directly onto the infected areas of your houseplants.

5. Tomato Spray

This spray helps in dealing with an aphid infestation through natural means. The magic component is 'Tomatin' that's found in Tomato plants, and works wonders for pest management through its antimicrobial, insecticidal, and fungicidal properties. It has also proven to have a variety of health benefits, so you should definitely try this spray out.

You'll need

- 4 cups of water
- 2 cups of tomato plants (fresh and clean leaves)

Method

1. Cut up the tomato leaves into small bits.
2. Mix them up in water and let it sit for 12-24 hours.
3. Strain the leaves out.
4. Transfer the water into a spray bottle and use it on infected houseplant leaves for pest control.

6. Soap and Orange Citrus Oil Spray

Slugs are another relatively common houseplant pest which didn't quite make the list in this chapter. Nonetheless, if you're dealing with a slug problem, this spray could come in handy! It also works well against other invasive pests like ants and roaches.

You'll need

- 1 oz orange oil
- 1 gallon water
- 3 tbsp castile oil

Method

Stir all ingredients together and transfer the mixture into a spray bottle. Use it on your infected leaves, and remember to shake well before use for maximum effectiveness.

7. Garlic and Onion Spray

This list already has a garlic spray at the top, but it's even more potent when combined with the helpful properties of onions. These two aren't just the magic ingredients in the kitchen, but apparently also in your home garden! It also keeps well for about a week before losing its potency if you store it in the fridge.

You'll need

- 1 onion
- 1 clove of garlic
- 1 tbsp dish soap
- 4 cups of water
- 1 tsp cayenne pepper

Method

1. Mince the onion and garlic (by hand or otherwise) and mix the paste with water.
2. Let it sit for an hour before adding dish soap and the pepper.
3. Mix well and move it into a spray bottle to treat bug-infested areas.

[**Warning:** Make sure you test all store-bought or homemade solutions thoroughly before fully exposing your plants to them. This is because some sprays or pesticides (both, homemade and store-bought) can have adverse reactions with some plants and cause severe damage.]

BEST WAYS TO PREVENT HOUSEPLANT PEST INFESTATION

So far, we've only discussed *corrective* measures for each of the above insects, which means you can perform them *after* your plants have already been infested. However, there are solutions that can also take care of these problems *before* they even occur — which makes them *preventive* measures.

There are many practices you can perform to lower the risk of pest infestation in your garden or indoor plants. They aren't foolproof by any means, but they've proven to be effective and mostly sufficient to keep plants safe from many kinds of pests.

So, here's what you should do to significantly reduce the possibility of having to deal with an annoying houseplant pest problem in the future:

1. Use clean soil mix and pots

Most pest problems arise from poor hygiene in terms of forgetting to thoroughly clean the pot before setting up a new plant in it. Ideally, you should clean your pots with a bleach solution or diluted soap to make sure it's free of any germs or harmful bacteria.

You should also try to get a new bag of soil mix (or make a fresh batch at home) for your new plants to dodge the possibility of fungal matter or leftover eggs overwintering in the soil from previous pest infestations.

2. Inspect a new plant well

Before you buy a new green friend, make sure to give it a close look to make sure it doesn't bring any unwelcome guests into the house. Since most types of pests are invisible to the naked eye, many novices make the mistake of buying already-infested plants, bringing them home, and spreading the problem all over their collection.

To avoid that, it's important to observe new plants as carefully as possible before buying and bringing them home. If you notice and identify harmful insects, not only should you avoid them, but also bring them to the shop owner's attention. This allows them to quarantine the plant in time to prevent spread and also prevents them from selling it to some other oblivious novice.

3. Maintain a safe distance between plants

We all became aware of the term "social distancing" over the last few years — thanks to the COVID-19 pandemic. Well, the thought behind that was to keep people at least 6 feet apart, reducing the chances for people to share airborne germs through breathing.

Similarly, you should also maintain a safe distance between your houseplants as a preventive measure against pest infestations. Ideally, no plant's leaves should be in contact with the leaves of another! While this won't hinder the spread of winged pests (like fully grown aphids), they'll still limit the mobility and spread of wingless insects (like scales).

4. Clean off pests from the plant's soil ball

Even if you checked the plant closely before you bought it, its soil can sometimes be filled with surprises. Sometimes, it'll be home to pests like sow bugs, roly-polys (pillbugs), and even millipedes — they all thrive in dark, damp conditions.

Such insects aren't necessarily harmful to plants, but they'll eat away the decaying organic material in the soil. However, some experts consider millipedes harmful pests for houseplants as they eat away tubers and bulbs.

If you find millipedes in the soil of a newly bought plant, you can deal with them by spreading Diatomaceous earth. They're fossilized diatoms that kill millipedes by cutting— breeding and replicating within them. Quite disturbing to think about, but hey, as long as it works. You can also capture the ones you spot and set them free outside.

5. Keep your new plants isolated for some time

Many novice houseplant owners make the rookie mistake of buying a new plant for their home and adding it to their indoor collection straight away. The risk factor there is that sometimes, store-bought plants can be very recently infected by pests, which means they'd have little to no symptoms when you purchase them.

The new plant might seem healthy, but it might still have pests (or their eggs), which puts the health and survival of all of your other plants at risk. So, you should always keep a new plant isolated from your home collection for a few days (or even a couple of weeks) to see if it's safe to be an official new member of the family.

5

SPOTTING FUNGUS DISEASE

"In some Native languages the term for plants translates to 'those who take care of us.'"

— *ROBIN WALL KIMMERER*

I n previous chapters, we've learned about correctly fulfilling a houseplant's basic needs like light, soil, and water and protecting it from external threats like pests. Unfortunately, pests aren't the only thing to keep an eye out for — there are many other risk factors that are just as dangerous to your plant's wellbeing (if not more). A prime example is fungal diseases and their spread. It's essential to know what they are, their common types, and how to keep your plants safe from them.

After reading this chapter, you'll be equipped with the basic intellectual arsenal to detect, identify, and treat common fungal diseases in a timely manner to prevent their spread to other healthy plants.

FUNGUS PREVENTION HACKS

It all starts with prevention — because what's better than the disease not happening in the first place?

You can prevent fungal diseases by making the conditions as unfavorable for them as possible. While the humidity and temperature preferences vary amongst different fungi types, they mostly show up and thrive in humid conditions with a lack of open airflow.

Considering that, here are a few preventive measures you can take to keep fungal issues away from your plants:

1. Avoid overwatering by always checking the soil's moisture level before each watering session. As mentioned in previous chapters, you can check it by inserting your fingers about an inch or two into it and checking for moisture. If it's there, hold off on the watering can.

2. Since limited airflow encourages fungal growth, you should ensure healthy ventilation around the plant and maintain good aeration in your soil. Houseplants shouldn't be crammed up into a single room. Even adding a fan to your indoor houseplant setup can help prevent fungi by stimulating airflow.

3. Perform regular drainage checks on all your plants and don't let them get waterlogged. Since moisture buildup is the mother of fungi, waterlogging is the last thing you need in your houseplants (which is when there's too much water stuck in the plant's root zone due to poor drainage).

4. Another tip to avoid moisture buildup in your plants is to water them in the morning instead of doing it in the evening or at night. That's because the sun is a great natural evaporator of the excess water off of the plants and soil, and you'd miss out on that by watering in the dark hours.

5. You can also keep spraying your plants with anti-fungal sprays (homemade or store-bought) periodically to prevent fungal outbreaks. A water and baking soda mixture is one of the simplest and most effective DIY sprays you can make. It disrupts the ion balance of fungal cells

and prevents spores — but we don't need to get into all the scientific jazz, all you need to know is that it's easy and it works!

6. Don't leave dead plants or dropped leaves lying around for too long as they can rot and lead to fungal growth.

MUSHROOMS | *NOT BAD*

It's not uncommon for mushrooms to pop up out of the soil of houseplants if owners fail to maintain preventive measures. For instance, plants kept in humid, warm, and poorly ventilated rooms are at the highest chance of mushroom growth. It all starts from spores that find their way in through clothes, air, or the soil mix itself — and if the conditions are favorable, they grow and pop out!

The most common variety in the case of houseplants is yellow mushrooms — but luckily, they're totally harmless to plants. In fact, you actually wouldn't mind their presence at all since they play a somewhat positive role by breaking down the soil. It's fine to let them live their life and coexist with your plants. However, many plant owners like to remove them since they have pets and children who could try and swallow them.

If that's the case with you, or you just have minor OCD and can't stand mushroom growth in your houseplant soil — here's what you can do:

- Pull mushrooms out gently by their stems and carefully throw them away. Try not to shake any more spores out of them into the pot while you're at it.
- Make the conditions drier, colder, and more aerated.
- Scrap out the top layer of your soil and dispose of it to get rid of any spores that may be lying around. Add a fresh layer of sterile potting mix on top.
- If the mushroom "problem" persists, repot your plant.

SOOTY MOLD | *PRETTY BAD*

Unlike yellow mushrooms, sooty mold is a real cause of concern. It's a black fungus that's a gift from unwanted visitors like aphids, scale, and whiteflies. These pests secrete clear honeydew, which is where sooty mold grows from.

Sooty mold is by no means harmless to your houseplants. It forms a covering on the surface of their leaves and blocks out their exposure to sunlight. As you can imagine, that interferes with photosynthesis — i.e., the bread and butter of your houseplants. As a result, they can suffer from symptoms of stunted growth and decoloration.

Here's how you can deal with sooty mold:

- The first step is to target the source of the problem. In this case, it's pests (and the honeydew they secrete). Start by identifying the type(s) of pest(s) thriving in your houseplants, and take pest-specific measures to get rid of them as soon as possible.

(The previous chapter has covered all three pests that give rise to sooty mold, including ways to identify and get rid of them.)

- Wash the affected plant leaves using a hose. But be gentle! You don't need to give those leaves a pressure wash; just a steady flow of water is generally enough to knock pests off.
- Spray a non-toxic pesticide or neem oil all over the leaves of an affected plant, also reaching for cheeky spots (like stem cooks, nodes, and underneath the leaves). It's advisable to take your indoor plants outdoors for this little activity if you don't want to stink up your

home. You'll have to repeat this a few times to
see noticeable results.

- Once you've successfully gotten rid of the pests,
you've successfully addressed the source of the
problem! Now, to easily clean off the actual
sooty mold — wipe the leaves with some water
and dish soap, and that should do the trick.

POWDERY MILDEW | *BAD*

If you ever find a white layer of something that looks
like icing sugar or flour at the top of your houseplant's
soil, that's powdery mildew — and it's bad news. The
problem starts with airborne fungal spores and spreads
pretty quickly all over the plant (and eventually to other
nearby plants if left untreated).

This fungal disease thrives in conditions with a lack of
light exposure and poor airflow. It's seriously
dangerous to a plant's health (and life) since it can cause
a plant to drop leaves, weaken, and deform.

Let's hope your precious plants never encounter it —
but if they do, here's what you need to do:

- To make sure that the fungal disease doesn't
spread out to other healthy plants, the first step
is to set the affected plant at a safe distance

from all other houseplants. Its new spot must be properly ventilated with sufficient light exposure.

- Next, cut out all the leaves with powdery mildew.
- Spray the plant with a fungicide for houseplants (following all instructions mentioned on the label).
- Regularly wipe the plant's leaves with soapy water to keep the problem from recurring. This also helps keep insects away.
- Lastly, remember to wash your hands right after you've handled a plant with a fungal disease. This is to prevent fungal spores from making their way to your healthy houseplants through channels like your hands or clothes.

WHITE MOLD | *OKAY-ISH?*

White mold isn't harmful to your plants (hence the "just fine" tag above), but it's still a sign that your houseplant might be missing out on some of its needs. If you spot white mold on your plant, it means the plant could have better ventilation, lighting, and moisture control.

On the bright side, it's not something that weakens or damages the plant. However, in the case of indoor plants, it's still a cause of concern for you as you don't want to breathe mold in — do you?

Here's how you can get rid of white mold:

- Put a mask on and scoop out, and get rid of the top layer of affected soil using a trowel. Make sure you get all the visible mold out. If there's too much mold, it might be worth repotting the plant altogether in fresh, sterile soil.
- Sprinkle some cinnamon powder over the soil as it's a natural fungicide that prevents mold growth!
- Make sure to optimize the plant's environment with light, healthy air circulation, and precise watering to keep fungal issues away.

GRAY MOLD (BOTRYTIS) | *BAD*

Unlike white mold, gray mold (or Botrytis) is a real cause of concern for your plant's wellbeing. Common symptoms include the flowers, stems, and leaves of the plant developing a gray-ish tan.

The gray spores of this fungal variation prefer relatively cool temperatures and high humidity. An effective preventive measure would be to make sure your houseplant leaves do not remain wet for a long time after each watering session. You can ensure this by simply watering in the daytime to make sure any excess moisture on the leaves gets quickly evaporated.

Gray mold hits the plant's old parts the hardest, using a broken leaf or stem as its entry point. However, this one's a fast spreader and can significantly harm your houseplants if left untreated.

So, here's what you need to do:

- Start by isolating the plant to make sure the fungal disease doesn't make its way to other plants.
- Cut out all moldy parts of the plant, including leaves and stems. Also scrape out a layer of the soil if there's visible mold on it. Discard everything carefully and avoid getting it on your clothes. Wash your hands, tools, and clothes afterwards.
- Move the plant to a spot with conditions that are unfavorable for gray mold — i.e., somewhere with less humidity, warmer temperature, and good ventilation.
- On a cloudy day, take the plant outdoors and spray it with a fungicide while closely following the instructions on it. Bring it back in once it dries up.

- Remember that dropped and dead leaves, flowers, and stems are the primary food source of the mold — so, keep cleaning up and removing these from your plants regularly. You can also get in the habit of dusting any accidental cuts (or broken stems) on your plant with cinnamon powder to prevent mold buildup.

FUNGAL LEAF SPOTS AND RUST | *BAD*

Spotted leaves is a common symptom in houseplants indicating that something's wrong, but it could be a lot of things. For instance, it could be overwatering, sunlight damage, mineral deficiencies, bacterial damage, or fungal damage.

Spotted leaves from fungal disease occur as a result of airborne fungal spores sticking to a wet leaf of your houseplant in warm conditions. It all starts from a tiny bump in the leaf (formed by the spore), which expands into a much larger spot. The problem spreads out and covers the entire leaf if left untreated. It can even spread to the stems and branches.

Fungal leaf spots can be of many different colors depending on the species of fungi that are causing them. Common examples include tan, yellow, black, white, and reddish-brown.

A plant might also have rust spots, which are unique fungal leaf spots that show up as orange-red blisters underneath the leaves, and bumpy, red spots on their surface. It generally causes leaves to warp and drop. However, this variation has a higher chance of occurrence in outdoor plants than indoor ones.

Here's how you can treat fungal leaf spots:

- Start by isolating the plant to protect its "neighbors" and place it in a cool, dry place with good air circulation around it.
- Snip away the spotted leaves and carefully seal them in an airtight back to prevent spread.
- Try not to mist or overwater the plant, and don't leave any residual water sitting on its leaves after. Make sure the plant's stem and leaves dry out well in bright, indirect light after a watering session.
- Take the plant outdoors on a cloudy day to spray it with some fungicide solution. Let it dry out well and bring it back inside and repeat this process several times.

CROWN, STEM, AND ROOT ROT | *VERY BAD*

Crown, Stem, and Root Rot occurs due to fungal mycelia that can coexist with your houseplants in their soil. The fungus can very quickly spread out and multiply in the right conditions — which in this case, would be limited air circulation, overwatering, and cool temperatures.

Here's how you can effectively deal with crown, stem, and root rot:

- If you can see rot at the stem or anywhere above the soil, cut those sections out and sprinkle the cuts with fungicide powder (or cinnamon powder).
- Watch out for overwatering! Try to always check for moisture in the soil before watering and always water your plants in the morning. Also, avoid getting any water on the plant's leaves or stem.
- You can also try repotting your plant using fresh soil that's dry and sterile. While you're at it, get rid of as much of the old soil as you can from the roots, and remember to sterilize your new pot.
- Lastly, this fungal disease isn't easy to fight off. So, if the plant still doesn't show any signs of

recovery, you might want to take some healthy cuttings at the top and try to propagate (discussed deeply in the next chapter).

In this chapter, we've gone over the essential tips to prevent fungal diseases in your houseplants, the various types of fungi threats to look out for, and how to treat them. You should do everything you can to prevent fungal diseases, but if they do occur, it's important to act quickly. That's because they can spread like wildfire if left undetected (and hence untreated) for a long enough period.

Luckily, there are a lot of well-researched techniques to help a houseplant that's suffering from a fungal disease. Still, if all else fails, you can always try propagating some of the plant's healthy cuttings to give it an all-new shot at life — baby Groot style! The next chapter is all about that, so read on!

6

PROPAGATION AND REPOTTING
101

"Plants are more courageous than almost all human beings: an orange tree would rather die than produce lemons, whereas instead of dying the average person would rather be someone they are not."

— MOKOKOMA MOKHONOANA

S o far in this book, we've already covered most of the stuff you need to know to have a surface-level understanding of how to look after your houseplants. But, this is where things get a bit more advanced — and equally exciting! In this chapter, we'll have a brief look at processes like

- Propagation (& tips)
- Cutting
- Division
- Layering
- Grafting
- Budding
- Repotting

Some of the above procedures, like repotting, are essential to give your plants a fighting chance against pest infestations and fungal infections. Similarly, propagation allows you to expand your houseplant collection without having to buy anything from the nursery! Essentially, you'd take a few cuttings and set it up in its own pot to grow into a big boy — and the cycle goes on.

You can even use propagation as a backup plan when you're treating an infected plant. All you need is a few healthy cuttings planted in a separate pot which will continue to thrive and grow even if you fail to save the original plant.

So, the contents of this chapter are pretty important — to say the least. Let's get into it!

PROPAGATION FOR BEGINNERS

Who doesn't want to expand their houseplant collection? Good news — you could do it right at home without having to spend an extra penny on new buds, seeds, or even a greenhouse. Even though the word propagation starts with "pro," it's actually pretty newbie-friendly! You don't need any pricey equipment either. All it takes is an ounce of love for plants, the will to learn, a little patience — and yeah, some essential supplies.

With the propagation techniques shared in this chapter, you'll soon have the next generation of your houseplant collection sprouting out!

What's Plant Propagation?

In simple words, reproducing a plant from a single plant parent is a process called propagation.

This primary goal of reproduction can be achieved through many different techniques which all fall under the umbrella of propagation. Examples include budding, grafting, division, and the most common one — cutting. Each technique has its own pros, cons, and risk level (cutting being the lowest risk of them all).

But before we break down each technique, let's address a quick question — **what sets plant propagation apart from regular plant reproduction?**

Well, while regular plant reproduction production involves seeds (containing genetic material from two plant parents), propagation is an asexual alternative to reproduction that only requires a single plant. Moreover, while seed-started plants give birth to all new plant babies, plant propagation leads to new, semi-mature, plants. Not only does that make the process faster, but also has a much lower risk of failure.

Now, let's discuss popular propagation techniques one by one and the steps you can follow to try them out.

Cutting

The cutting technique involves "cutting" off a healthy stem of the plant you want to propagate, and potting it in fresh potting soil. Depending on the nature of the plant, you can also propagate it in water. For instance, most Aroid plants like pothos, monsteras, ZZ, and philodendrons can all be propagated in water as their natural environment and ancestral background is swamps.

Even some land plants have tendencies to adapt, survive, and grow in the water. However, you'd want to propagate them in a soil mix for the best chances of success.

You need

- A plant to propagate
- A pair of scissors
- Garden gloves
- A water-filled glass vessel (room temperature)

✿ Step 1

Observe your plant to find a mature vine, and look right below the stem/vine juncture or the leaf to find little brown-colored root nodes. They'll be about an inch long. Snip off a few inches of healthy stem and make sure the cutting has a node or two on it as that's where the new roots show up.

✿ Step 2

Get rid of any leaves if you find any close to node(s) — especially if they're low enough to be under the water in your glass vessel.

✿ Step 3

Gently put the cutting in a glass vessel that's about halfway filled with room-temperature water. Make sure you place the vessel in a spot that gets sufficient indirect sunlight. Placing it directly in the sun (like on the window) is a rookie mistake that may lead to a much lower success rate depending on the type of plant you're propagating.

✿ Step 4

This is where you take a step back and let nature take its course. Practice patience and let the cutting grow on its own! Be sure to check back for a close observation every week or so to see how much the root has grown out of the nodes, top off the water if it looks a bit low. You could also replace the water from time to time, but it's not necessary as long as there aren't any visible signs of fungal growth or murkiness.

✿ Step 5

Once you see root growth that's about 1 inch long (or longer), you can also transplant the cutting into a potting mix. Typically, you'd get to this stage no sooner than 30-45 days.

Once you've successfully potted the cuttings in a soil mix, saturate it with water (again, room temperature) and place your pot in a spot that gets lots of indirect light.

Remember to check the soil for moisture before each watering, and apply all of the watering tips you've learned in previous chapters for healthy growth.

Division

Another technique for propagating plants is a process called "division" — which is most commonly used for propagating plants that have a lifespan of over two years. The right term for such species in planting jargon is "perennials."

The process entails digging up the plant's sight, dividing it, and migrating it to another pre-prepared spot. This way, each division gets plenty of nutrients and water with less competition for vital resources — hence promoting growth and rejuvenation for each half.

Division can be carried out in a rough or fine way. The "rough" version involves an axe or sharp blades to slash, cut, dig, and replant clumps of plants. On the other hand, sophisticated division practices consist of carefully digging the site, gently breaking the plant's clumps apart by hand, and using a sharp knife to cut them apart.

Layering

In the layering technique of propagation, the "new plant" remains attached to its single parent for a certain period as it grows new roots after a modification in the mother plant's stem structures.

Other methods of layering

Layering has 5 different types:

- Simple (discussed above)
- Tip
- Compound (also known as "Serpentine" layering)
- Stool (or mound)
- Air

✿ Simple

Simple layering involves winding and bending a mature branch of the parent plant down into the ground. Using ground staples, the branch is pinned in place with a cover of soil on top — with a 6 to 12-inch section with the shoot tip left uncovered. From there, the process of root development starts to take its course. Once the new roots emerge and fully develop, the branch is severed from the "mother" and continues to grow as an independent plant.

Simple layering has a high success rate with plants like abelia, boxwood, honeysuckle, forsythia, climbing roses, wax myrtle, azalea, rhododendron, jasmine, and pyracantha.

✿ Tip

Similar to simple layering, except that the shoot tip is buried in a hole instead of being left above the ground.

You can try out tip propagation with plants like dewberries, raspberries, blackberries, and loganberries.

✿ Compound

Compound layering is also closely related to the base technique used for simple and tip layers. What sets compound layers apart is that the stem section is buried at several different points throughout its length, which exposes and uncovers the stem between those points.

At each section, one lateral bud must be buried and one left exposed.

This is a pretty advanced procedure of layering and you shouldn't try this out until you've been successful at several simple and tip layer attempts.

Once you do reach that stage, give it a shot with vine-type and trailing ground cover plants. E.g. willow, heart-leaf philodendron, rambler roses, grapes, pothos, wisteria, clematis, dogwood, viburnum, vining honey-suckle, etc.

✿ Stool (Mound)

The stool process of layering — also commonly referred to as "mounding" — takes place in several steps in a complete growing season. The first step is to cover the plant's base with substrates or soil (like mulch) which is left as it is for some time (several weeks, or even months) until there's visible root growth developing on the plant's shoots, arising from the main stem's buds.

From there, you cover half the plant's height in soil to let roots develop on lateral shoots. These shoots are cut away from the main stem when new roots start to form. At that point, you plant the cutting separately and it (hopefully) grows into a new plant!

Nurseries commonly use this technique for fruiting trees to propagate dwarf understocks. However, it's one of the trickiest methods of propagation with the most number of steps involved. You'd better push this way down your bucket list of houseplant adventures to make sure you tackle it with some respectable layering experience under your belt.

✿ Air

Lastly, we have air layering. In this variation, you target a branch that's somewhere up the middle of the trunk but still within reach. Ideally, its diameter should be between 1 to 2 inches. A bigger branch works best in terms of layering success chances.

Once you have the ideal branch in sight, try to make a vertical cut in the stem's upper part as well as two horizontal ones over and under the vertical one. Once the cuts are in place, peel the bark off around that entire area. Apply some auxin to stimulate faster root growth.

Once you've done all that, wrap it all up with moist peat moss and some plastic (as if you're bandaging a bruised finger). Make sure that it's wrapped well by securing it with a rubber band or some twist ties.

Soon, the growing roots should develop and penetrate the moss which you'd be able to spot through the plastic wrap. Once you see that occur from all sides of the branch, it's time to cut the branch right underneath the roots (without damaging them) and plant it.

You can try this procedure out with roses, dracaena, Oregon grape holly, magnolia, dumb cane, croton, schefflera, azalea, rubber plant, Norfolk Island pine.

Grafting

Along with cutting, division, and layering, you can also propagate plants by grafting! It involves cutting off one plant's twig and attaching it to another's stem. This way, they form a unit and function as one. The process is relatively complex, yet it's one of the most effective ways to get the desired combination of qualities and character to your plant. It's almost like the planting version of selective breeding!

Pro tip: *Make sure to use clean gloves, or at least wash your hands well with soap before coming into contact with the plants to avoid transferring infections to the plant(s) along the way.*

The first question is when you should start grafting. Well, the actual process should ideally begin in spring, but you can begin your preparations in the dormant season, too — i.e. late winter.

Simple cut some new-growth scions that have buds attached, and store them in an airtight container (or plastic bags) in the fridge till spring. Once you get to that point, follow these steps:

✿ Step 1

The first step is to inflict vertical incisions on the bark of the rootstock. Start at the top and make 3-inch long cuts on four sides, and put a rubber band under the cuts. Peel off the bark on all four sections that are separated by the incisions (as if you're peeling a banana). Use the tip of your knife to make this easier, but be careful not to detach the four flaps!

After peeling the bark, cut off a 3-inch piece of the rootstock using shears.

✿ Step 2

Now that the rootstock is ready, it's time to prepare the scion to go in it.

Trim the scion about half an inch near the bottom to reveal green, fresh wood. Slice its bottom end with a 2-inch cut to expose its cambium tissue that helps carry sap through the plant.

Create four evenly-spaced cuts using the same process.

✿ Step 3

Now it's time to connect the two! Carefully place the scion into the rootstock between the flaps, lining up the cut ends of the scion with the flaps.

✿ Step 4

Tightly wrap the graft with plastic and secure the joint in place using rubber bands. The key is to make sure the scion's and rootstock's cambium tissue is aligned and pressed against each other.

For additional protection, you can add a layer of aluminum foil before wrapping it up with plastic. Once the plastic wrap is on, put masking tape over it for 100% security.

Ideally, new buds should show up within a month (and sometimes even two weeks). It's a good idea to write the grafting date on the masking tape to keep track, especially if you carry out the process with several plants simultaneously.

Budding

Lastly, you can also propagate plants using the budding technique. It involves inflicting a cut in the rootstock, splitting it open to fit another bud into it — such that they form a unit and grow as one.

✿ T-Budding or Shield Budding Propagation

Shield budding is a propagation technique that involves making a shallow incision on the bark of a rootstock in a T shape (hence the name). When done right, the bar flaps hanging out of the T-shaped cut will lift away from the tree slightly, allowing you to slide the scion (in this case, a single bud) under them.

The scion for T-budding is generally a healthy bud that's carefully selected and cut out of the plant being propagated. Once inserted under the bar flaps, it must be secured in place by wrapping some grafting tape or thick rubber bands over the closed flaps — over and under the scion.

✿ Chip budding propagation

Chip budding is another variation of the budding propagation technique. In it, you cut the rootstock plant at an angle between 45 and 60 degrees, with a right-angle cut under it. This lets you cut a triangle-shaped chip out of the rootstock plant. In the same way, you'd also cut the scion (or the bud) out of the plant being propagated and place it in the triangular cavity of the rootstock plant. Once it's inserted, it's secured by grafting tape.

PROPAGATION TIPS

Now that you know what propagation, its types, and step-by-step processes are — make sure you remember the following tips when you try any of it out.

Cutting preparation tips

The "cutting" is an essential part of any propagation technique, as that's what eventually grows into a new plant — or goes into the rootstock plant to propagate. Here are some tips to get it right.

- Every plant is different, so make sure you follow specific instructions and advice depending on the plant you wish to propagate. The "right" steps may vary from plant to plant, and a quick Google search will let you know if your method of propagation works for that plant, and the modifications you need to make to the procedure (if any).

- Try to get your cutting from a fresh, new, and healthy part of the plant.
- Don't let dropped leaves from the cutting float around in the water as they can pollute the water as they rot with time.
- You can use rain or filtered water if you choose, but tap water also works just fine.
- Your cutting's spot should have plenty of indirect light, but not direct sunlight. If there's a window in your home that doesn't get direct sunlight, but sufficient indirect daylight, that'd be a perfect spot for your propagation cuttings to grow.
- Don't place your cutting in an extremely hot room as that speeds up rotting.
- You can mix seasol or rooting powder into the water to stimulate faster root growth in propagation, but it isn't necessary — especially if you don't want the water to look murky.

Maintenance tips

- You should replace the water in your glass vessel at least every two weeks. Keep an eye on it and regularly top it up if it looks low, and change it out sooner if it starts looking murky.
- Before you transplant your cutting from the water vessel to the potting mix, make sure it's ready — with roots that are at least an inch or two long.
- Remember that you can't wait too long to transplant your cuttings from the water to the soil. That's because, after a long time, the roots may get used to the water and go into shock upon being transplanted to a potting mix.
- Some plants can survive and even grow in water permanently, but might need a bigger vessel with continued root growth. You should also add some fertilizer into the water after certain intervals to make sure the water is sufficiently nutrient-rich to sustain the plant's growth.

WHERE TO FIND CUTTINGS

As mentioned above, cuttings are the most important part of any propagation procedure — no matter what technique you use. So where do you get them?

Well, the easiest (and most cost-effective) source of cuttings is one of your own houseplants. However, some people propagate for the sole purpose of increasing the plant variety in their home collection — which means they obviously won't have it in the first place. If that's the case with you, you can always request a cutting from your neighbors if they have it.

Thanks to the internet, you can join online houseplants groups and ask for a cutting on forums to see if someone has it near you (maybe even in exchange for one of your own plant's cuttings). The community is close-knit and generally very helpful, so it's definitely worth a shot.

As a last resort, you can always visit your local nursery and buy a cutting of the plant you're looking to propagate.

PLANTS RECOMMENDED FOR WATER PROPAGATION

Some plant cuttings propagate better in a water vessel than potting mix. Here's the list!

Vine Plants

- Syngonium
- Swiss cheese plant (Monstera Adansonii)
- Golden Pothos (Devils Ivy)
- Variants of Pothos like Marble Queen, Snow Queen, Satin
- Fruit salad plant / Monstera Deliciosa
- Monstera Siltepecana
- Heart Leaf Philodendron (Philodendron Cordatum)
- Peperomia Scandens
- Philodendron Micans

Leaf Cuttings

- Cacti (and many succulents)
- Snake plant
- Begonia
- Peperomia family of plants (like Watermelon, Emerald Ripple, Obtusifolia)

Stem Cuttings

- Chain of hearts
- Burro's Tail / Donkey's Tail
- String of pearls/bananas/beads
- Fiddle Leaf Fig
- ZZ plant
- Maranta (cut under leaf node)
- Woody stemmed succulents (most of which can be snipped from anywhere along their stem)
- Coleus (cut below node)

From a bulb or seed

- Avocado
- Hyacinth

Pups

- Chinese money plant
- Spider plant

Some plants don't respond to water propagation at all. Some examples are the Peace Lily, Calathea, Ferns, Palms, etc.

The best thing you can do before your propagation attempt is to google the plant and look at its advised technique and tips for propagation.

HOW TO REPOT A PLANT

Spring is a great time to repot your plants into fresh soil as they're ready to grow faster than ever after a sleepy winter! Besides seasonal repotting, the practice can also come in handy to treat issues like waterlogging or simply as a necessary step in procedure propagation.

Here's a step-by-step guide to correctly repot your plants!

✿ Step 1

The first step is to gently remove the plant from its current pot. Now, that certainly is easier said than done. The difficulty level may vary depending on the type of plant you're working with. Some are attached more firmly at the base of their pots, while others slide out relatively easier when you tip them over.

For those firmer plants, you'll have to slide a small shovel down the sides to detach it from the walls (even a butter knife or a spatula works great) and keep at it until it softens and slides out. If the pot is somewhat malleable (like the ones made out of plastic), you can also give it some gentle squeezes to loosen its hold.

When the plant begins to slide out, grasp it around the sides and wiggle/slide its pot off. Make sure to keep your grip as gentle as possible.

Inspect the bottom of the plant to see how badly your plant need repotting! Most plants with poor drainage will have their roots jumbled up into a circle at the bottom which means they were waterlogged.

✿ Step 2

These jumbled-up roots need to be freed out to be able to take advantage of healthy aeration and proper water/nutrient absorption. All you need to do is gently massage the circled bunch of roots at the bottom, "caressing" it with your fingers until you feel them loosen up.

Not all roots will make it to their new home as some will fall out during the loosening process, but that's fine. As long as you're not aggressively breaking off any roots and pulling on them — you're doing it right.

By the end of your massage session, the roots will no longer be tied up together and have plenty of room to freely breathe, drink, and grow!

✿ Step 3

The plant's new pot should ideally be about an inch or two larger than the previous one. The roots should have sufficient wiggle room, but not too much as an extra-large pot will surround the roots with excess soil. This means they won't be able to absorb all the moisture between waterings — leading to root rot. It'll only waterlog your plants again, which is one of the most common reasons behind houseplant death.

So, get an appropriate-sized pot and fill it up to about one-third capacity with fresh soil (ideally a potting mix that's suitable for the type of plant you're repotting). Then, place your plant in the middle of the plant and hold it up — keeping the stem base about half an inch below the pot's top. Make sure the plant is at the right height by removing or adding the soil underneath it.

From there, add potting mix around the plant as you gently hold it in place. Fill up all of the pot's empty spaces, fill it up, and lightly pat the soil down to make sure the plant is snugly fit.

✿ Step 4

Remember that plants that have been newly transplanted into a new pot will suffer from temporary stress — they're living things, after all! To deal with it, they need lots of water right away. If you've been paying close attention to your watering habits before, you need to be even more careful moving forward — your plant needs it!

For the first watering in its new home, place it inside a saucer or a cachepot (to catch drained water) and water the plant slowly. Let it all soak into the fresh soil, and start watering again until the pot starts to feel significantly heavier. Once you see water draining out of the pot's holes at the bottom, stop watering.

Let the plant sit inside the saucer for about 30 minutes as the roots absorb excess water to their fill. After that, take the pot out — place it in a nice spot with plenty of indirect lighting and good aeration, and empty out the cachepot.

Congratulations, you've successfully repotted your plant in the perfect manner! Doesn't it look a little greener already?

CONCLUSION

In this chapter, you've learned lots of new concepts — including the meaning, importance, types, and process of propagation. You've also learned the step-by-step process of repotting a plant in the best way possible, correctly its waterlogged roots along the way.

Both practices discussed in this chapter — propagation and repotting — are incredibly crucial for dealing with common houseplant issues like fungal infections and pest infestations. Now you know exactly how to do them!

Now, propagating is evidently a pretty advanced chapter in any houseplant enthusiast's journey, so it makes sense if you don't want to try it out right away. However, it's an essential concept to learn about — and we've all got to start somewhere. Now that you know what it is and how it's done, you at least know what it's for and how you can get into it when you feel like it.

7

THE BEST PLANTS FOR YOUR DESK

"Love and work are to people what water and sunshine are to plants."

— *JONATHAN HAIDT*

We've basically covered all you need to know about the basics of plant care, and how to prevent and treat common problems that may arise along the way. The following chapters in this book will expose you to many classifications of plants that are ideal for different types of parents.

In this particular chapter, we're talking about the best plants to sit on your desk! If you've never had that idea before, it's time to give it a serious thought. That's because plants can make your workspace feel much more tranquil, peaceful, and warm. They can make the spot feel more engaging and have a positive impact on your mood.

However, if you don't have much of a green thumb — which, no offense, is just a nicer way to say "lazy plant parenting and a lack of relevant knowledge" — desk plants can wither quite easily.

Luckily, we've compiled a list of the 10 ideal desk plants you can choose from, and how to take care of each one. They are:

- Devils Ivy
- Chinese Evergreen
- Weeping Fig
- ZZ Plant
- Bromeliads
- Heartleaf Philodendron
- Peace Lily
- Dragon Tree
- Snake Plant
- Creeping Wood Sorrel

We've handpicked each one of them aiming for qualities like easy caretaking, and being better suited to a workspace environment. Let's begin!

1. DEVIL'S IVY (*EPIPREMNUM AUREUM*)

The Devil's Ivy (Epipremnum Aureum) is also sometimes referred to as Pothos, even though that's technically not the same plant.

Devil's Ivy has big leaves, some of which can appear heart-shaped in different shades of green. It's pretty easy to care for, and makes for an ideal indoor houseplant to place on a wall shelf, a table, or your work desk.

✿ Lighting needs

The devil's ivy isn't too light-hungry. It's actually pretty sensitive to light, and won't tolerate being exposed to direct sunlight — or even extremely bright indirect light for the entire day. A darker space might slow the plant's growth down, but there's still room to adapt and it's safer for the plant. Aggressive lighting can easily burn its leaves and hurt the plant.

✿ Watering needs

Only water your devil's ivy when half of its soil is free of moisture in the summer, and when all of it is dry in the winter. Depending on the conditions, watering gap durations will vary but it's generally once a week.

❀ Ideal pot size

A devil's ivy doesn't need much space to grow — a regular 200mm-sized nursery pot would do.

❀ Potting mix

Since it's an easy plant to grow and take care of, many different potting mixtures can work — as long as they maintain proper aeration and drain well. A standard premium mix is probably your best bet, but you can also get away with an orchid or cacti mix if you have a bag or two lying around.

2. CHINESE EVERGREEN (AGLAONEMA)

Next up, we've got the Chinese Evergreen plant which is also called the Aglaonema. Their popularity comes from the unique color of their leaves which have a bright outline or traces of red or silver. The plant's scientific name breakdown consists of two Greek words — *aglaos* and *nama* — meaning "bright" and "fountain" respectively.

General Maintenance

While the Chinese Evergreen isn't too picky of a plant, it still has its specific needs.

✿ Don't Overwater

Check the moisture level in your Aglaonema's soil before each watering. You can use a soil probe for it, or just your finger. Only give the plant a drink when there the soil is dry at least a couple of inches down in bright conditions, and completely dry (all the way to the bottom) in lower-light conditions. These specifics are important, as you can easily over water the plant which causes root rot, and turns its leaves mushy or yellow.

✿ No Cold/Hot Air Drafts

Be careful not to have your work desk exposed to any drafts of hot or cold air, which can come from the window, electric heaters, and even air conditioning. You can still have the AC/heater on in the room, as long as there's no wind directly blowing over the plant, and the thermostat is set to somewhere between 70 to 85 degrees Fahrenheit (the ideal temperature range for Chinese Evergreen).

✿ How Often Should I Fertilize My Plant?

We recommend using organic fertilizer for houseplants and refreshing the potting mix with it every 6 weeks or so.

✿ How Often Does My Plant Need to Be Repotted?

Like most other small, desk plants — the Chinese Evergreen should be repotted at least once every 12 to 18 months.

3. WEEPING FIG (FICUS BENJAMINA)

The Ficus Benjamina — widely known as the Weeping Fig — is an eye candy plant species that can effortlessly boost the decor in any workspace. It comes from the tropical Southeast Asian, Indian, and Australian forests. Its scientific name is derived from the Indian acme Ben-ja.

General Care

✿ Water

Only water the plant when the top one or two inches of its soil are completely dry, with regular checks for drainage issues and water logging.

❀ Fertilizer

In the summer and late spring, liquid feed is recommended for healthy growth.

❀ Temperature

55 to 85 degrees Fahrenheit.Farenheit

❀ Repotting

Figs don't need to be repotted after regular intervals unless there's an issue like difficulty to water or waterlogged roots.

4. ZZ PLANT (ZAMIOCULCAS ZAMIIFOLIA)

Next up, we've got the Zamioculcas Zamiifolia — commonly referred to as its abbreviation "ZZ" (understandably so). The name might be hard to pronounce, but the plant is relatively easy to look after!

The plant stores quite a bit of water in its naturally bulging and fat roots, which means you don't have to water it every day. They're also not super light-hungry, and can safely spend hours without any bright light exposure. So, if you're guilty of "forgetting" to carry out essential plant care chores on time, the ZZ plant can be a perfect match for your desk.

It barely gets any pest problems and doesn't need much fertilizer to get by — making it the dream plant for beginners!

As a bonus, it acts as an air purifier to keep your workspace fresher naturally!

Warning: Toxic!

According to a NASA study, the ZZ plant can remove many toxins from the air like benzene, toluene, and xylene! However, every part of this plant is poisonous. Goes without saying, keep it out of the reach of pets and children, wash your hands after coming into contact with it, and don't consume it (or any toxic plant, for that matter).

General Care

❧ **Potting soil**

Any potting soil with good drainage.

❧ **Fertilizer**

Use a balanced houseplant liquid fertilizer with a 20-20-20 composition once a month.

❧ **Light**

Low to indirect light.

✿ Watering

Very infrequent — only water the plant when it's fully dry.

Propagating the ZZ plant

To propagate a ZZ plant, you'll have to separate their thick rhizomes (that look like potatoes), and replant them as the plant grows out of these. Growth is faster and more likely when several large-sized rhizomes are replanted together.

You can also snip a ZZ cutting with a bit of stem and two leaves on it and replant it.

5. BROMELIADS

If aesthetics matter the most to you, flowering plants like Bromeliads make the most sense! Like any other blooming plant, Bromeliads need a bit more attention. They're also pretty late bloomers, so you'll have to be patient, too — but their beautiful flowers and bright colors make it all worth it in the end!

✿ Water

You could get away with underwatering Bromeliads as they're naturally adaptable to drought conditions. However, they're sensitive to overwatering and can quickly develop root rot. That's why they need smooth drainage and a regular check for waterlogging. Don't water the plant unless its potting mix is dry at the top (at least two inches).

✿ Humidity

Ideally, bromeliads should be placed somewhere with around 60% humidity. It's the same for both, outdoors and indoor bromeliads.

That number is a bit high to maintain indoors at all times, especially if you live in a cold place that requires furnace heating. However, you can use the following solution to boost humidity:

- Humidifier near the bromeliads.
- Placing several other plants near bromeliads to boost humidity through transpiration.
- Keeping a spray bottle near your desk to mist the plant occasionally throughout the day.

✿ Pots and Potting Media

Since bromeliads are prone to overwatering (and hence root rot), it's important for its pot and potting mix to make up for this weakness. For instance, you shouldn't use plastic pots as they hold moisture for a much longer time. On the other hand, clay pots are porous and let water out to keep the plant safer from excess moisture between waterings.

As for the potting media, you should never use soil for bromeliads as it's too dense and doesn't offer the quick drainage that this plant needs. Rather, use potting media that's particularly made for bromeliads, or make a DIY mixture using plenty of porous materials for quick drainage.

✿ Light

Not all bromeliads are the same when it comes to lighting tolerances and preferences. Some variations thrive in indirect, bright light — while others need to be shaded at all times.

However, bromeliads mostly prefer sunny, bright conditions. But, like most other plants, extended exposure to direct sunlight can damage the leaves.

✿ Fertilizing

This is one area where bromeliads aren't as high-maintenance. They don't need much external fertilization at all, aside from an occasional boost with a water-soluble one that's diluted to about a half or quarter strength. Instead of the plant's central tank, you want to fertilize around its base. Be careful not to overdo it though, as it can potentially make the leaves leggy and diminish their colors' vibrance.

✿ Flowering

If you get all of the above conditions right, soon, bromeliads will reward you with bright red bracts with some inflorescent purple accents. The bloom lasts for a few months with gorgeous flowers that can light up your workspace!

6. HEARTLEAF PHILODENDRON (*PHILODENDRON HEDERACEUM*)

The Heartleaf Philodendron is one of the most popular members of the Philodendron family. They produce dark green waxy leaves generally in the shape of a heart. Like the devil's ivy, this plant also shares many characteristics with the pothos plant.

Steps for Planting Philodendron

1. Get a pot with some drainage holes to reduce overwatering risk.
2. Use a potting mix with good drainage with ingredients like perlite or sand in it.
3. Find a spot with sufficient indirect bright light for your heartleaf philodendron.

4. Water it every 14 days (yes, this plant is one of the least thirsty ones out there).

5. Regularly snip away the dead leaves to keep your philodendron from getting leggy.

6. Keep a close eye on pests since this plant is prone to infestations of aphids, spider mites, and mealybugs.

7. If necessary, spray your plant with some diluted liquid dish soap or neem oil to fight pests (or prevent them).

8. Fertilize it monthly, using a suitable water-soluble fertilizer.

✿ Repotting

Heartleaf philodendrons don't need repotting after a certain interval. Instead, you can do it as needed if the plant outgrows its container or simply gets waterlogged.

7. PEACE LILY

The peace lilies are one of the prettiest houseplants out there, and they surely deserve a spot on your desk — especially if you're looking to elevate the aesthetic of your workspace. The plant has broad, wide, dark green leaves with gorgeous white flowers during bloom.

These plants don't need a ton of light and aren't very sensitive to overwatering. As a bonus, they'll also clean the air in your room and remove toxins to make your environment fresher naturally.

Note: Remember that peace lilies have calcium oxalate in all their parts — which means they can cause respiratory and stomach problems upon ingestion. This makes them mildly toxic and you should keep them well out of reach of curious children and nibbling pets!

Planting, Transplanting, and Dividing Peace Lilies

- Get an all-purpose potting soil mix with good drainage but some ingredients that help retain some moisture between waterings (as peace lilies don't do well in soil that's completely dry).
- You should repot the plant every couple years in the bloom period to allow it to benefit from fresh soil in the spring.
- Whenever the plant outgrows its pot, you can divide it. For this, simply remove the peace lily from its container, split it into smaller sections, and replant them. As long as you leave a few leaves on each clump, each section will grow into a full-sized peace lily plant!

Can You Grow Peace Lilies in Water?

If you've visited your local nursery recently, you might have seen peace lilies on display in vases with no soil! That's because these plants can grow well in water, too.

If you want to keep them in water at home, make sure you keep the plant's base suspended over the water using small river stones. This way, the roots can grow down into the water without getting the plant's base constantly wet (which is the formula for root rot).

Ideal Care for Peace Lilies

❀ **Watering**

The soil should always be slightly moist to the touch. While short periods of dryness are fine, the plant lets you know when it's thirsty as the leaves start to droop. When that happens, test the soil's moisture level, and if dry, give it some filtered water.

❀ **Humidity**

This plant prefers a high humidity level that's similar to the bromeliads discussed above. You can apply the same techniques here to maintain high humidity near the plant.

❀ Fertilizing

Peace lilies don't need too much fertilizing as they aren't heavy eaters. An occasional boost every 6 weeks is enough as it nears late winter.

❀ Temperature

60 to 70 degrees Fahrenheit.

❀ Lighting

Peace lilies prefer spots with sufficient bright, indirect light throughout the day. An east-facing window is ideal.

How to Address Flowering Problems in Peace Lilies

If your peace lilies aren't flowering, it most probably has to do with lighting. While these plants aren't necessarily too needy when it comes to light, they won't bloom desirably in complete shade throughout the day! If their current spot doesn't get much indirect daylight, move the plant to a location that does and let it sit there for at least a few hours a day before moving it back to your desk.

Moreover, if you encounter flowering issues, you should only use a fertilizer that is specifically meant for flowering plants to avoid problems like less volume, or weak-looking, green flowers.

8. DRACAENA

The dracaena, also known as the Dragon Tree, is one of the most aesthetically pleasing indoor plants out there. It has red-edged leaves with sharp edges.

It's pretty easy to look after which makes it an ideal pickup for house-planting novices with a keen eye for beauty! It's drought tolerant (so you can get away with forgetting to water it) and it's super hard to kill.

General Care

✿ Water

This plant has high drought tolerance. It's also pretty easy to overwater it, so make sure that the top half of the soil in its pot is dry when you water it. The general ideal gap between waterings is a few weeks or so.

✿ Light

Dracaena prefers bright light but not direct (as that can easily burn the foliage).

✿ Soil

Use a loose potting mix with great drainage to prevent overwatering.

✿ Temperature

Ideal temperature for this plant is between 70 and 80 degrees Fahrenheit.

✿ Humidity

Regular humidity is fine for the Dragon Tree, but you should give it an occasional mist with a spray bottle if you've got furnace heating going on (or just have a particularly dry environment inside the house for some reason).

✿ Fertilizer

The plant doesn't rely on fertilizer for healthy growth, but you can still top it off with a balanced liquid fertilizer at the beginning of spring.

Pruning Dracaena

Like most other plants, the dragon tree isn't immune to shedding. Whenever you spot a dead (or dying) leaf, quickly pick it up and discard it. Give the plant an occasional trim to tidy it up and get rid of some leaves that look like they're on the verge of falling off. Make sure to use a sterile tool to prune your plant!

Propagating Dragon Tree

If you like to propagate your plants, the dragon tree is going to be one of your favorites as it's super easy to propagate!

All you need to do is

1. Get some sharp, sterile scissors and snip off a long piece of the stem (about 8 inches).
2. Get rid of the leaves attached to the stem.
3. Plant the cutting in potting soil and place it in a spot that gets indirect, bright daylight. Make sure you remember which end goes into the soil and don't make the rookie mistake of planting the cutting upside down!
4. With time, you'll see leaves sprouting out on the cutting's upper nodes — and you've got a brand new Dracaena baby growing!

Potting and Repotting Dragon Tree

You can repot Dracaena into a larger container if it starts to outgrow its pot. However, this is a pretty rare instance as these plants are pretty slow growers, which means you won't have to repot them for at least a couple of years. However, you can still do it regularly just to refresh its potting soil right before spring season.

9. SNAKE PLANT (SANSEVIERIA TRIFASCIATA)

The Snake plant — scientifically called Sansevieria trifasciata — possibly has one of the funniest nick-names in the entire houseplant realm. It's commonly referred to as the "Mother-in-law's tongue," and you can make of that what you will!

Nevertheless, it's a gorgeous-looking plant that can easily add a ton of visual value to your workspace interior. It's also one of the hardest plants to kill, capable of surviving in low light without a month of watering. It can even handle being exposed to direct sunlight for long periods!

General Care

✿ Light

Snake plants can easily survive in most lighting scenarios. However, they prefer indirect yet steady lighting with some time in direct sunlight.

✿ Soil

Loose potting mix with good drainage.

✿ Water

Once a month (or whenever the soil dries out).

❀ Temperature

The best temperature range for snake plants is between 70 to 90 degrees Fahrenheit. Cold conditions are the plant's weakness and can kill it.

❀ Fertilizer

Use mild cactus fertilizer at the start of the growing season with a 10-10-10 composition.

Pruning

Use a sterile pair of scissors to cut away damaged leaves, or foliage growth near the soil line. The ideal time to do this is right before spring kicks in to prevent stressing out the plant. The plant gets quite tall if left unchecked, which isn't ideal if you're keeping it on your desk. You can always snip off the taller leaves to keep the plant's height manageable.

Propagating Snake Plant

You can easily propagate snake plants in the growing season (summer or spring). The best way to do it for this plant is division, which we've covered in detail in the previous chapter *"Propagation and Repotting 101."*

Growing Snake Plants From Seeds

You can also grow this plant from seeds, but it's significantly tougher than propagating it by division. That's because its seeds have a very low rate of germination and take up to a month and a half before there's a seedling in sight.

To do it, you have to:

1. Fill the seed starting mix (or cactus potting mix) into a small pot.
2. Sprinkle snake plant seeds on top.
3. Cover it up with clear plastic.
4. Keep the soil slightly moist throughout this period.
5. Put the pot in a sunny spot and wait three to six weeks before you spot a seedling.
6. Remove the covering and repot the seedling when it's about four inches tall.

Potting/Repotting Snake Plants

Make sure to pot snake plants in a container made up of sturdy material as this plant's roots can easily break the weak ones. As mentioned above, this plant rarely needs repotting due to its slow growth but the best time to do it is spring. Always stick to cactus mix or potting media that's particularly made for snake plants for best results.

10. CREEPING WOOD SORREL (OXALIS CORNICULATA)

The Oxalis make up 800 of 900 species of the Oxalidaceae family — being the largest genus in it. It contains flowering plants with over 550 species that are native to the tropical forests of South Asia and South America.

These plants are excellent houseplants because they're colorful, grow fast, and spread like wildfire! In fact, they're so easy to spread that greenhouse growers and gardeners see them as invasive weeds — but that doesn't mean you can't light up your desk's aesthetic with them!

General Care

✿ Light

This plant prefers bright, indirect to direct daylight. It doesn't thrive in shade or low-light conditions.

✿ Water

Only water them when the top half of the soil is dry, which takes about 1 to 2 weeks depending on lighting conditions.

❀ Humidity

Regular room humidity is ideal.

❀ Temperature

The plant thrives in temperatures between 65 to 85 degrees Fahrenheit.

❀ Soil

Suitable soil contains garden substrate and organic matter with good drainage.

❀ Fertilization

Fertilize the plant in the fall season with a slow-release product or compost.

The creeping wood sorrel doesn't need pruning, but you might have to get your scissors out every once in a while just to keep their fast growth and spread in check! They are considered invasive plants after all. However, they're naturally resistant to diseases and pests.

Propagation

You can propagate these plants by dividing rhizomes (similar to the ZZ plants propagation discussed above) or by sewing their seeds in spring.

CONCLUSION

All of the plants covered in this chapter are ideal for desktop placement. Each one of them has been carefully picked out for two key qualities: how easy it is to look after them, and how big of an impact they have on improving your workspace, your mood, and even the air quality in the room.

But do you know that there are plants that are even easier to take care of? You can basically forget about watering them for weeks and they'll still be fine. You guessed it; succulents! The next chapter is all about them, so keep reading!

8

TOP 10 SUCCULENTS

"We are made for loving. If we don't love, we will be
like plants without water."

— *DESMOND TUTU*

This chapter is all about succulents, and the best ones you can adopt as a beginner in the world of houseplants! It takes a deep look at the following plants, including the general care guidelines for each one and a foundational understanding of their needs and preferences. It covers the following 10 succulents:

1. Burro's Tail
2. Crown of Thorns
3. Flaming Katy
4. Jade Plant
5. Aloe Vera
6. Panda Plant
7. Pincushion Cactus
8. Roseum Plant
9. Zebra Plant
10. Hens and Chicks

Known for their long lifespans and low maintenance, succulents are great for even the busiest plant parents. Some of their key benefits are

1. **They're highly adaptable.** Succulents are able to grow in almost any climate condition.
2. **They're natural air humidifiers.** These plants release moisture into the air and help with common sickness symptoms like dry cough, cold, sore throat, and dry skin.
3. **They oxygenate the air.** Having succulents breathing inside the home will naturally enrich your indoor environment home with fresher oxygen.
4. **They have natural air purifying qualities.** According to one NASA research, succulents

are able to get rid of many VOCs (volatile organic compounds) from the air — which is a remarkable health benefit.

5. **They expose you to many benefits of exposure to nature.** Some examples include improved cognitive memory, heightened pain tolerance, and sharper memory. Sounds unbelievable? You'd be surprised that all of these benefits were found as a result of reliable research studies held at reputable institutions like the University of Michigan, and the University of Kansas.

Even if you're not into those science-y benefits, succulents are also one of the best-looking plants out there! They're a top choice for many wedding and event planners these days as a way to elevate the look of a venue with some natural class and elegance.

So, we've established that succulents are amazing plants to have around the house. Let's take one step further, and have a look at our 10 handpicked succulents that maximize these benefits with the least amount of effort required to look after them.

1. BURRO'S TAIL (SEDUM MORGANIANUM)

The burro's tail is often followed by the word cactus in many articles and publications, but it's technically a succulent. Fun fact, all cacti are succulents, but not all succulents are cacti!

The Burro's Tail is also called a donkey tail plant and takes very little attention to survive and grow.

Propagation

This plant has small, round leaves, and long stems. You'll commonly find some of its fallen on the ground around it. Luckily, you can use these leaves to propagate the plant by inserting them partially into a soilless, moist medium. Keep it moist until you see it root out, after which you can repot it as a new burro's tail plant!

General Care

✿ Soil

It needs sandy, dry soil to thrive. A cactus mix is a safe bet.

✿ Container

It requires a container with excellent drainage through specs like a porous material (e.g. terracotta), and large drainage hole(s) at the bottom.

✿ Watering

With sufficient lighting, the plant only needs watering once every two weeks.

✿ Light

It needs direct, bright light. Remember to keep turning it to evenly expose all angles to sunlight for balanced growth and to avoid sunburn.

Don't Overwater

Like most other succulents, the Burro's Tail is highly susceptible to severe damage from overwatering. There's a high chance of developing root rot, especially in plants that haven't matured yet. Besides disciplined watering, the right soil type and container type will also help alleviate overwatering risks.

2. CROWN OF THORNS (EUPHORBIA MILII)

Crown of thorns is a flowering succulent originating from Madagascar. It's also called "Christ thorn" or "Christ plant," and blooms colorful small flowers. It's also really spiny! The branches contain milky sap which comes out when you break them. The whole plant is also toxic, which means it should be kept away from children and pets.

How to Grow Crown of Thorns

You can grow this plant from seeds, but only during a specific time of the year. It's also quite a slow germination process, so propagation is a great alternative. Follow these steps to propagate the Crown of Thorns.

1. **Snip your cutting(s).** Ideally, it should be cut about 3 to 6 inches from the tip of one of the plant's leafy stems.
2. **Dry them.** Once you've obtained your cuttings, it's important to let them completely dry off in a cool place. It can take a few days but don't skip this step as the moisture in fresh cuttings can lead to root rot.
3. **Plant dry cuttings.** The ideal potting mix for this plant consists of compost, sand, and peat. Get your dried cuttings and bury the rooting end, setting them up so that they stand firmly. Give it a drink, and a new succulent life has begun!

General Care

✿ Temperature

65 to 75 degrees Fahrenheit.

✿ Sun

About 3-4 hours of direct sunlight every day.

✿ Watering

In the summer, only water when there's no moisture in the top inch of potting mix. In winter, water your crown of thorns when there's no moisture in the top three inches of soil.

✿ Fertilizer

Liquid fertilizer — every 2-3 weeks in summer, spring, and fall.

You should also keep a close eye on your crown of thorns for pest infestations and fungal diseases as the plant is susceptible to both of those risk factors. As we've learned in previous chapters, detecting these problems earlier on provides you a better shot at treating and saving your plants with timely measures.

3. FLAMING KATY (KALANCHOE BLOSSFELDIANA)

The Flaming Katy is a unique succulent that has some of the most breathtaking flowers among all blooming succulents. Come spring, you'll see gorgeous clusters of multicolored, delicate flowers ranging from orange, red, white, pink, yellow, and purple shades. They only last a few weeks, but they're certainly a sight to behold.

How to Get Flaming Katy to Bloom

The plant should reward you with adorable flowers if you check the following boxes:

- Give the plant generous sunlight for a few days at the beginning of the blooming season, followed by shorter hours of daylight. This sets up flower buds.
- For the first 2 weeks of October, make sure the plant stays in a dark room for about 13-15 hours every night, only giving it moderate amounts of sunlight during the daytime.
- Don't fertilize and water minimally during this period.
- Following these steps, you should see bloom buds appear within 2 months. At that point, you can get back to providing regular care.

General Care

✿ Light

Several hours of direct sunlight or continuous indirect, bright daylight.

✿ Water

The soil mix should barely have any moisture, as the plant is susceptible to overwatering and root rot. Only water when the top inch of soil is dry.

✿ Humidity

Regular room humidity (about 40%).

✿ Temperature

65 to 80 degrees Fahrenheit.

✿ Soil

1 part perlite and 2 parts regular potting mix.

✿ Fertilizer

Start feeding the plant with a water-soluble balanced fertilizer from late spring with one-month intervals.

To propagate the Flaming Katy plant, take its stem cuttings near the end of spring and follow the same process as the Crown of Thorns' propagation.

4. JADE PLANT (*CRASSULA OVATA*)

The jade plant is another flowering succulent that's super easy to grow, look after, and propagate. It has a thick trunk, with a branch structure that makes it look like a mini-tree. Its leaves are shiny, thick, and have a deep green shade. In some variations of the plant, the leaves are oval-shaped with bright red outlines!

When it blooms, it develops gorgeous star-shaped flowers featuring an eye-catching combination of pink and white.

General Care

❀ **Water**

Don't let the soil dry out completely, and water it as soon as the top soil feels dry.

❀ **Light**

Full direct sunlight, all day.

❀ **Temperature**

65 to 75 degrees Fahrenheit during the day, and 50 to 55 degrees Fahrenheit at night. However, they can still survive at much higher temperatures as long as they get sufficient sunlight during the day.

❀ **Fertilizer**

Every 6 months, fertilize your jade plant with a balanced fertilizer that's water-soluble.

✿ Pruning

Regularly prune your jade plant and snip off dead or shriveled branches.

It's also super easy to multiply your jade plants through propagation! Just follow the same procedure described above for the Crown of Thorns' propagation which involves breaking off a piece, letting it dry, and planting it into the potting mix with some fertilizer in it.

5. ALOE VERA

The most popular succulent on this list (and possibly in the whole world) — we've got Aloe Vera. It's one of the most common houseplants in most parts of the world, mostly due to its miraculous medicinal uses. You'll find it in all sorts of products made to ease burns, reduce inflammation, skin lotions, cosmetics, and ointments. Some people even like to consume the gel in its leaves raw, which has a variety of proven health benefits.

How to Grow Aloe vera

The simplest way to grow aloe vera is to snip a healthy cutting and plant it in a suitable potting mix. However, the most successful (and quickest way) to grow it is through division and pups.

This requires repotting the parent aloe vera plant. Remove it from its current container, brush away rock and soil from the plant's root system at the base, and carefully cut a healthy pup with a few roots using a sharp knife. Lay it in a warm, dark room to let it dry off for a few days (allowing it to callus on the end to prevent root rot). Once the pup's end is dry, pot it in some gritty potting mix and wait for the roots to start growing before watering it. Place the pot in a spot with bright, indirect light — and you're set!

General Care

✿ Light

Bright, indirect sunlight.

✿ Soil

Well-draining, gritty soil mix (any cactus potting soil works).

✿ Water

Don't let the soil dry out completely and water your aloe plant regularly whenever the top 1 or 2 inches of soil are devoid of moisture. Overwatering and under-watering can both cause aloe leaves to turn yellow, shrivel, and die.

❀ **Temperature**

55 to 85 degrees Fahrenheit.

❀ **Humidity**

40% (normal room humidity).

❀ **Fertilizer**

Doesn't require much support from a fertilizer. An annual boost with a standard houseplant fertilizer should be plenty.

❀ **Pruning**

If you spot any brown tips on any of your aloe plant's leaves, prune off the affected section using sterile shears. Be careful not to prune the leaves in the center of your aloe plant.

6. PANDA PLANT (KALANCHOE TOMENTOSA)

The Panda Plant is an interestingly named succulent that's titled after its small, fuzzy, velvety-appearing leaves. They have reddish-brown markings on the edges that add to the plant's beauty. The plant is native to Madagascar, and is super-low maintenance due to its high adaptability. It can survive indoors for years!

General Care

✿ Water

The plant doesn't need too much water. Water sparingly — and only when the soil feels dry at the top — to prevent root rot.

✿ Temperature

60 to 75 degrees Fahrenheit.

✿ Fertilizer

In the growing season, use a diluted fertilizer every month or so till summer lasts.

✿ Repotting

Repotting is not necessary, but you can do it if it's needed due to root rot or container outgrowth.

✿ Pest Control

Panda plants are susceptible to mealybug infestations so make sure you keep an eye on the plant. If you do spot some mealybugs, quickly remove them with rubbing alcohol wrapped cloth.

If you'd like to make more of these plants to add to your indoor collection, you can try propagating them during the growing season! Simply pluck some healthy leaves off of the parent plant and root it into a perlite mixture or a sandy cactus potting soil. Soon, you should see new roots and leaves develop. Once you get there, repot it into a new container.

Remember that the entire plant is toxic to animals, so keep it out of the reach of your pets.

7. PINCUSHION CACTUS (*MAMMILLARIA CRINITA*)

The pincushion (mammillaria crinita) qualifies as both, a cactus and a succulent — and has pointy, sharp spikes all over it. It's been found in many southwest areas of the US, but the plant originates from Mexico. It has a maximum height of 6 inches, making it a pretty manageable-sized succulent to add a desert feel to your interior decor!

Flowering Pincushion Cactus

This succulent has a party trick up its sleeves; an occasional bloom! When the stars align, and all of the plant's watering and climate conditions are met within an ideal range, it may surprise you with some flowers in spring season. You can increase your chances by cutting off your watering for a few weeks right when spring starts to start the buds. It might also help to provide the plant with cactus food to make sure it has enough nutrients to bloom flowers.

General Care

✿ **Water**

Like all other succulents, the pincushion cactus has high overwatering risks. Let the top part of the soil completely dry out before you give it another drink.

✿ **Temperature**

50 to 75 degrees Fahrenheit.

✿ **Soil**

Cactus growth potting mix with excellent drainage.

✿ **Fertilizer**

Use a cacti-feed formula every two weeks during spring to fertilize the pincushion cactus.

✿ **Light**

Direct sunlight, full-day, all year round.

Propagation

You can propagate the Pincushion Cactus in one of two ways:

1. **Offsets (pups):** Use gardening gloves and gently pluck off offsets from a healthy mother plant. Let the cutting dry up for a couple of days and

repot it in a cactus starting soil mix with good
drainage.

2. **Seeds:** To propagate this succulent using seeds,
sow them on top of a cacti soil mix inside a pot.
Cover them up with a thin layer of sand and
keep the top layer moist. Let the pot sit in a
warm place for a few days at about 70 degrees
Fahrenheit.

The only downside with this method is that the germination process is a bit slow, and it only works in the
Sspring season.

8. ROSEUM PLANT (SEDUM SPURIUM)

The Roseum plant is another unique-looking succulent
that does well in planters, containers, or a windowsill
inside your home. It grows fast, and low – only about
four to six inches in height. In the summer, you'll see
gorgeous star flowers in shades of light pink which can
easily uplift your interior decor!

General Care

✿ Soil

Survives easily in any soil mix. However, you should
aim for a nutrient-rich soil mix with good drainage.

✿ Water

Can live in months of drought without watering. Under normal circumstances, watering it twice a month is sufficient — but watch out for wrinkly leaves as that's a sign of underwatering.

✿ Light

Can do well in both, partial shade and full sun.

✿ Temperature

Preferred temperature is between 65 to 75 degrees Fahrenheit.This succulent can survive freezing cold temperatures without a problem — we're talking even -20 degrees Fahrenheit! Most other succulents cannot handle frost at all.

✿ Fertilizer

The plant doesn't rely on fertilizer for growth, but a diluted 5-10-10 water-soluble fertilizer can still help during spring.

Propagating Rose Stonecrops

You can propagate this plant by cuttings, that way, you'll retain all their properties in the new plant. Growing them from seeds can lead to characteristic loss, such as a different color than the parent succulent.

9. ZEBRA PLANT (*HAWORTHIA FASCIATA*)

The Zebra Plant has one of the most striking appearances amongst all other succulents on its list, mostly because of the white stripes on its leaves (hence the name "Zebra"). Its leaves grow about 5-6 inches in both width and height — and can add breathtaking aesthetic value to any home interior.

General Care

✿ **Sunlight**

This plant needs direct, full sunlight.

✿ **Water**

When the Zebra plant gets sufficient sunlight, it only needs to be watered once every 2-3 weeks with plenty of time for the soil to dry out between each watering session.

✿ **Humidity**

Average ambient humidity is fine as the plant can also handle dry air.

✿ **Temperature**

65 to 75 degrees Fahrenheit.

Propagation

To propagate the Zebra plant, you have to follow the exact same process as the one described for Aloe Vera above.

It involves gently separating a haworthia bud from a parent plant, letting it dry in warm conditions for at least 24 hours, and potting it into the new, well-draining pot with a cactus starting mix. You should wait a week or so before watering it for the first time — and that's it!

10. HENS AND CHICKS (*SEMPERVIVUM TECTORUM*)

Last but not least, we've got the succulent with the oddest name on this list — Hens and Chickens (Sempervivum tectorum). But, there's a good reason behind it! It has nothing to do with the plant's looks but with its excellent ability to multiply and give birth to many "chicks." Even its scientific name — Sempervivum — means to "live forever." Even though the plant only lasts about 3 years, it brings enough chicks into the world to live through them forever!

General Care

✿ **Temperature**

65 to 75 degrees Fahrenheit.

✿ **Light**

Full sun (at least 6 hours a day).

✿ **Soil**

Sandy cactus soil mix.

✿ **Water**

Infrequent watering with intervals of several weeks to let the soil dry out in between. In warm climates, you can water it once a week if the soil dries out quicker.

✿ **Pest Control**

This succulent is prone to an infestation of pests like aphids and mealybugs so keep a close eye. If you spot any, remove them with a cotton swabswap covered in rubbing alcohol.

✿ **Fertilizer**

Not needed.

Propagating Hens and Chicks (Sempervivum tectorum)

Following the same procedure of separating offsets from a healthy succulent parent (as discussed several times above), move onto the following steps:

1. Transplant the hens and chicks offset into a quick-drain soil mix using a trowel, making a shallow cavity to spread out its roots.
2. Lightly water the offset, letting it dry out before you give it the next drink. From that point on, you should see plants spreading (or the 'hens' producing 'chicks') on their own), as long as the conditions are ideal.

Growing Hens and Chicks From Seed

You can also grow this plant through seeds, although that procedure is slower with slimmer chances of success. Simply sprinkle the seeds on fresh succulent potting mix that's set up in a small pot with a drainage hole. Moisten the mix lightly and place it in a location that gets lots of bright light. Give it about 3-4 weeks (assuming that it's spring with ideal climate conditions), and you should see some sprouting. At that point, you can add some mulch and gravel to the mix to stimulate it further.

Getting Hens and Chicks to Bloom

Unlike other succulents, blooming isn't necessarily a good thing with hens and chicks. These plants are grown for their foliage and their tendency to multiply quickly through self-propagation. In fact, flowering can very well be a sign of bad conditions for the hens and chicks plant. If you want to make it bloom flowers, you can deliberately stress the plant out by shading it and adding fertilizer.

CONCLUSION

This chapter has covered some of the easiest to look after, and the hardest to kill succulents out there. The best part about them is how they can go weeks without watering and little to no maintenance! They're the perfect choice of houseplants for people with a limited tolerance for additional responsibility, and a high tendency to forget waterings!

Succulents mostly provide aesthetic benefits. But, if you're the type of person who wants much more practical usage out of their houseplants, you should direct your attention toward plants that act as natural air purifiers! The next chapter is all about those.

9

BEST AIR PURIFYING PLANTS

"A plant needs to do more than stretch its leaves toward the sun. It also needs to send down roots deep into the ground. They hold on tightly in the dark, out of sight where it is easy to forget about them. But it is the fact that a plant can do these two things at once, anchoring itself to the earth even as it reaches for the sky, that makes it strong."

— CAMERON DOKEY

I n this chapter, we'll exclusively discuss the plants that have the best possible impact on the air quality inside your home. There are countless plants that can purify the air, get rid of harmful toxins, and reduce the risk of respiratory diseases like asthma for you and your loved ones.

Some good examples of such air purifying plants are:

- Barberton Daisy
- English Ivy
- Indian Chrysanthemum
- Spider Plant
- Broad Lady Palm
- Kentia Palm
- Rubber Plant
- Flamingo Lily
- Kimberly Queen Fern
- Peacock Plants

Many houses and buildings suffer from reduced air exchange due to amenities like better insulation and air conditioning. This leads to breathing the same air over and over again, and that's not ideal — especially since people spend the most of their time indoors.

Thankfully, that's an easy fix if you're already looking to get some indoor plants! Pick a few plants from the above list of air purifying plants, and you'll be exposed to the following benefits.

- **Plants can get rid of toxic contaminants.**
  Toxins in the air like benzene, toluene, and
  volatile organic compounds (VOCs) can easily
  give you itchy, sore eyes, nausea, headaches, and
  a reduced attention span. Plants can target all of
  those contaminants and make the inside of
  your home healthier — naturally!
- **They exhale oxygen and inhale carbon
  dioxide.** That's the opposite of what humans
  breathe in and breathe out, making plants the
  ideal "paying guests" to coexist with. In some
  studies, increased oxygen levels in the air have
  shown a direct rise in productivity and
  concentration.
- **Plants keep humidity in check.** Too much and
  too little humidity is bad. Plants tend to
  naturally keep it in control and bring it closer
  to the healthiest range for humans.
- **It's research-backed.** In a *"Clean Air Study"* by
  NASA, researchers found that many plants have
  a clear detoxifying effect on your home by
  getting rid of toxins, germs, and dust particles
  that may be airborne, or found on furniture.

With all those benefits, it's evident that every houseplant enthusiast should have at least a few air purifying

plants as part of their indoor collection. But which ones? Let's begin.

1. BARBERTON DAISY (GERBERA JAMESONII)

The Barberton daisy (Gerbera Jamesonii) is one of the best air purifying plants to target toxins like benzene, formaldehyde, and trichloroethylene inside your home. These contaminants commonly exist as part of "sick building syndrome" — which refers to the toxins that make their way inside home through modern synthetic construction materials including paints.

This plant also adds gorgeous shades of orange, red, and yellow and pink to your decor, making it one of the most beautiful indoor plants on this list. It's easily a must-have plant!

General Care

❁ **Light**

Needs sufficient direct sunlight.

❁ **Water**

As soon as the top of the soil feels dry, water the plant. Ideally, it should be somewhat moist at all times.

✿ Soil

Potting mix with peat as the main ingredients. Recommended formula is 1 part perlite and 2 parts peat.

✿ Fertilizer

During bloom, fertilizer the plant using a balanced liquid options — once every two weeks.

✿ Humidity

The plant prefers high humidity, but it should be fine at regular home humidity (around 40%).

✿ Temperature

55 to 75 degrees Fahrenheit.

Propagation

The Barberton Daisy is commonly propagated through seeds, but you can also expand your collection of this plant through replanting root cuttings.

Flowering

Unlike many flowering plants, the Barberton Daisy doesn't rely on spring season to bloom its gorgeous flowers (though it sure helps). At any time of the year, it'll reward you with flowers that are 3 - 4 inches wide, lasting about 4 - 6 weeks.

2. ENGLISH IVY (HEDERA HELIX)

The English Ivy (Hedera Helix) is another plant that's incredibly effective at purifying the air inside your home. It specializes in getting rid of airborne fecal particles, making it the best plant for your bathroom. It's an easy-growing perennial vine and has shown to fight the mold levels inside your home.

General Care

❀ **Light**

Part shade to full shade.

❀ **Water**

Prefers to be slightly on the dry side, so always make sure there's no moisture at the top of the soil before each watering.

❀ **Soil**

Well-drained, loose potting mix.

❀ **Fertilizer**

20-20-20 organic fertilizer, every two weeks during spring.

✿ Humidity

Loves high humidity, making it an even better fit for the bathroom.

✿ Temperature

Between 70 and 90 degrees Fahrenheit.

Pruning

Regular pruning of the English Ivy plant can prevent bacterial leaf spot, and also keep their size manageable. Make sure to use sterile and sharp shears.

Propagating

To propagate the English Ivy, you can find healthy stem(s) that are about 5 inches in length and submerge them in a container with water (cut ends down) in the conditions listed above. Wait for roots to develop and then repot the stems into the ground or pot.

Potting and Repotting

Since this plant has certain invasive tendencies, planting them into the ground isn't always a good idea as they're naturally fast spreaders. Most houseplant enthusiasts like decorating them in hanging pots, allowing them to droop over the sides for aesthetic reasons.

You can repot the smaller English Ivy plants once a year when spring starts, and the larger ones twice a year. Use fresh potting mix and add some organic fertilizer to ensure sufficient nutrition. You can revive older plants by repotting them into fresh mix, as well!

3. INDIAN CHRYSANTHEMUM (*CHRYSANTHEMUM INDICUM*)

The Indian Chrysanthemum (Chrysanthemum indicum) — also referred to as "chrysanthemums" or "mums" — is a flowering plant belonging to the Asteraceae family. They have gorgeous orange, red, yellow, white, or purple flowers — with large flower heads with countless small petals. Mums are easily one of the best looking plants on this list, but that's a subjective opinion!

Bloom Forms

Depending on the species and variety, they have five common bloom forms:

1. **Regular Incurve** - Florets of petals completely conceal the plant's center, forming a ball shape as they all curve inward.
2. **Single or semi-double** - There's one or two petal rows near the plant's center — resembling

daisies.

3. **Anemone** - Resembles a semi-double formation but with a larger, higher, and plushier center floret.
4. **Pompom** - This bloom form is relatively smaller where petal rows fully cover the plant's center.
5. **Spider** - Spider mums have tubular petals that are long with hooks at the end.

How to Plant Chrysanthemum Seeds

To grow mums from seeds, you should plant them in the spring.

It's best to let the seeds germinate indoors before transplanting them into your garden or a pot outdoors. Sow them into a potting mix that's rich in organic matter and has good drainage. You can also boost them with fertilizer (and standard mix). In about 10 to 15 days, they should sprout in warm conditions.

Once the seedlings are eight inches tall, they're ready to get transplanted into your garden. Make sure to pick a location with lots of direct sunlight.

General Care

While mums will bloom every year in spring, here are the conditions to keep them healthy throughout the year.

✿ Soil

Standard potting mix with good drainage.

✿ Pruning

To promote flower growth and bushier foliage, snip off the stem tips every month and maintain the plant's height at 6 inches tall.

✿ Pest Control

Mums can be affected by diseases like powdery mildew and pests like aphids. You can take precautionary measures like spacing them out, maintaining healthy aeration around them, and watering them close to the soil without getting the leaves wet.

✿ Water

The plant has a shallow root system so the top layer of soil should almost always be moist. Give the plant a drink when the top layer of soil looks to be almost dry, but ensure smooth drainage.

✿ Fertilizer

Any standard gardening fertilizer once or twice a month in bloom season.

Propagation

You can propagate mums in several ways. One is to grow them through seeds, and the other two are offset division and replanting cuttings.

✿ Offset division

For offset division, dig a healthy plant up along with its roots in the spring and separate them into several foot-wide pieces. Replant these in new pots (or new holes in the garden) and it's done!

✿ Cuttings

Another way is to cut off the top 4 inches of a healthy stem and plant it in a suitable potting mix (preferably made of peat moss and sand). Place it in a spot that gets plenty of bright, indirect light. It should take about 14 days for the roots to develop, after which you can replant it into a bigger pot — or in the garden outside.

4. SPIDER PLANT (*CHLOROPHYTUM COMOSUM*)

The spider plant is the ideal choice for newbies looking to improve the air quality at home. It's resilient, not too picky about conditions, and works in silence to fight harmful toxins like xylene and carbon monoxide. It's also non-toxic to animals so it won't be a threat to your pets.

General Care

❀ Light

Part shade — a bright window with indirect daylight is ideal.

❀ Water

Soil should be moist, but not too much. Spider plants are sensitive to chlorine and fluoride, so avoid using tap or mineral water. Rainwater works best, with distilled water as a substitute to it.

❀ Temperature

70 to 90 degrees Fahrenheit. Protect them from cold air drafts from air conditioners as they're sensitive to cold.

❀ Humidity

40 to 60%.

❀ Fertilizer

Granular all-purpose fertilizer — once a month during spring and summer.

✿ Pruning

Remove and browning or dead leaves in a timely manner.

Propagating

Mature spider plants can be propagated through **offset division** and **cutting replantation** in the same way that's described above for propagating mums.

5. BROAD LADY PALM (*RHAPIS EXCELSA*)

The Broad Lady Palm helps clear out ammonia levels in the air inside your home. Lots of cleaning products have it, which means almost every home is affected — unless they've got this plant to undo the damage! It's also quite pleasing to look at and relatively easy to look after, making it a worthy addition to this list.

General Care

✿ Temperature

60 to 80 degrees Fahrenheit.

✿ Light

Indirect daylight throughout the day. An east-facing window works best.

✿ Watering

Keep the soil slightly moist with consistent watering, but ensure proper drainage — both in the soil and the pot's drainage holes.

✿ Soil

Organic-rich soil with excellent drainage works best.

✿ Fertilizer

Once a year, enrich the soil with palm fertilizer.

✿ Humidity

50% or higher. You can maintain this by keeping it close to other plants and/or placing a humidifier near it.

Propagation

The broad lady palm is a relatively expensive plant to get your hands on — so why not propagate it? It even makes for a great gift if you've got any friends who share your love for houseplants, or are planning to get into it.

The best way to propagate the broad lady palm plant is to replant a healthy cutting. Simply snip it about 6-8 inches from the tip, and carefully trim the leaves on the lower end of the step using a sharp blade. Place it in a water jar and wait for root development. Every 2-3 days, replace the water and keep the jar in a spot that gets plenty of daylight for best results. The roots should establish completely within 2 weeks, after which you can transplant it to your garden or a pot, maintaining all of the conditions described in the table above for healthy growth.

6. KENTIA PALM (HOWEA FORSTERIANA)

The Kentia (or *Thatch*) Palm is one of the world's most popular indoor palms. It's a flowering plant that can grow as tall as 10 feet in the right conditions and with proper care. It's got everything you'd want in a beginner-friendly plant – being cold tolerant, shade tolerant, and a natural air purifier!

General Care

✿ Light

Aim for at least 6 to 7 hours of indirect sunlight.

✿ Soil

Any well-draining pot mix works as the plant isn't picky about soil.

✿ Watering

Water your kentia palm once a week as it's susceptible to root rot. Cut back on your watering if you notice

204 | MICHE FERRET

yellowing leaves, and bump it up in case of brown leaf tips.

❀ Temperature

About 55 degrees Fahrenheit.

❀ Humidity

It benefits from higher humidity so give it an occasional mist spray, or place the pot on some rocks to boost humidity.

❀ Fertilizer

Use control release potassium supplement fertilizer.

7. RUBBER PLANT *(FICUS ELASTICA)*

Here's an unusual-looking Southeast Asian native – the Rubber plant (Ficus elastica). The plant's oval leaves give it a distinct (and easily identifiable) look. In its tropical habitat, it can very quickly grow as tall as 100 feet. However, they're commonly kept as an indoor plant for their air-purifying benefits, with regular cutting and pruning to keep their size manageable.

General Care

❀ Light

Give it lots of diffused, bright daylight.

✿ Soil

Rubber plants prefer a slightly acidic, well-drained gardening mix.

✿ Watering

Rubber plant requires frequent watering to retain sufficient levels of moisture. Check the first two inches of the soil and give it some water if it feels dry and crumbly.

✿ Temperature

60 to 75 degrees Fahrenheit.

✿ Fertilizer

Use a light liquid fertilizer throughout spring.

Propagating

The most common way to propagate rubber plants is by using leaf-tip cuttings. However, the method is pretty tricky, and not advisable for beginners. You're much better off buying a potted plant from your local nursery.

Repotting

In suitable conditions, a rubber plant grows pretty quickly. You might have to repot it several times until it reaches your desired height. Though it gets tougher to repot as it grows bigger (for obvious reasons) so if you can't move the container, simply shovel out several inches of soil from the top and add fresh potting mix in its place!

8. FLAMINGO LILY (ANTHURIUM ANDRAEANUM)

The Flamingo Lily has South American origins. It's another popular indoor plant with heart-shaped, dark green, shiny leaves! In the blooming season, it'll decorate your home with glossy bright, red spathes and yellow spadices in the middle.

General Care

❀ **Light**

Medium indirect light.

❀ **Water**

Re-water when the top two inches of soil are completely dry.

❀ **Humidity**

Try to maintain 80% humidity by placing the plant on a pebble tray or keeping a humidifier nearby.

❀ Temperature

70 to 85 degrees Fahrenheit.

❀ Fertilizer

Slow-release fertilizer.

❀ Repotting

Should be repotted every two years right at the start of spring (or whenever they are pot-bound).

❀ Cleaning

You can give the plant a shower every 1-2 months, gently rinse the leaves and prune away the discolored or dying ones.

9. KIMBERLY QUEEN FERN (*NEPHROLEPIS OBLITERATA*)

The Kimberly Queen Fern is known for its sword-shaped fronds. The plant grows big and upright with gracefully arching leaves – and it's commonly kept outdoors in warmer climates. However, it's also a common indoor houseplant – mostly for its striking looks, but also for its air-purifying qualities!

General Care

✿ Light

Partial sun to low-light conditions. Keep them near a bright window with indirect daylight.

✿ Soil

Rich potting mix with peat for good drainage.

✿ Water

Let the top 1 to 2 inches dry out before re-watering, which should take about 1-3 days (depending on heat and light).

✿ Temperature

60 to 70 degrees Fahrenheit.

✿ Humidity

70%.

✿ Fertilizer

Apply a balanced liquid fertilizer during spring and summer (once a month).

10. PEACOCK PLANTS (*CALATHEA MAKOYANA*)

If you appreciate the unique patterns and striking foliage in your plants, and can live without a bloom during spring, the Peacock plant is for you! It's not the easiest to care for, which means it's not the ideal choice for novice houseplant parents. But, if you *do* manage to get the conditions just right – it'll be one of the most impressive-looking plants in your home collection.

General Care

✿ Light

Filtered light or part-shade.

✿ Soil

Potting medium with some water retention and also good drainage. The recommended mixture would be one with sand, peat, perlite and organic matter.

✿ Water

Poke the soil each time you water the plant to make sure that the top one or two inches are dry. Watering should be very infrequent in the winters, so you might want to use a moisture meter!

✿ Temperature

60 to 75 degrees Fahrenheit.

✿ Humidity

Between 50% to 60%.

✿ Fertilizer

Feed the plant with diluted liquid fertilizers every two weeks during the growth period.

Propagating Peacock Plants

The easiest (and most popular) way to propagate peacock plants is through division. It's not easy though, so you might want to be prepared for a failure or two if you haven't done it before.

For the best chances of success, wait until the plant has grown into a large, well-established clump. Keep the repotted divisions warm, moist, and humid, and let them take their time to establish. If the environment might be too dry where you live, covering it up with some polythene sheeting can help retain humidity!

CONCLUSION

Air purifying plants is the best way to get some benefit out of your planting hobby! By getting rid of the toxins, contaminants, and even some nasty fecal matter in the air, the plants listed in this chapter will repay you for your time, money, and hours of hard work.

While there are many other air-purifying plants out there, most of the above plants were picked for their low maintenance and better compatibility with novices. Even if you miss a day or two of watering, or can't manage to maintain the precise levels of humidity, these plants let you get away with it and won't die on you!

Speaking of which… did you know that some plants are so easy to look after that they're basically impossible to kill? That's what the next chapter is all about!

PLANTS THAT ARE IMPOSSIBLE TO KILL

"A dried plant is nothing but a sign to plant a new one."

— *PRIYANSH SHAH*

I n this chapter, we're taking an in-depth look at the following plants.

1. Silver Pothos
2. Ponytail Palm
3. Moth Orchid
4. Christmas Cactus
5. Umbrella Tree

6. Cast Iron Plant
7. Hindu Rope Plant
8. Purple Shamrock
9. Kaffir Lily
10. Parlor Palm

Every person with plants at home has concerns about preventing or treating issues like overwatering, under-watering, pests, and root rot. But the biggest fear – the thing that all of these minor problems could potentially lead to – is a plant's death. Novices (and even seasoned houseplant hobbyists) always have this fear at the back of their minds, and rightfully so!

I remember back in the day, we had some relatively high-maintenance plants in the house and I'd look after them very carefully. But I had to go out of town for a few weeks and gave my mom a few pointers and directions to ensure their proper upkeep during that period. But oh well, my mom – bless her – did everything as carefully as she could, only to have me come home to a dying bird's fern nest, and a banana plant with badly browning leaf tips.

So, being new to the houseplant game, it's completely normal to experience a few failures when you're just starting off. The slightest issue can determine a fatal fate for your plants – depending on your climate conditions and the type of plants you've got. However, the best way to ease into this hobby without a depressing chain of plant deaths is to pick highly survivable plants!

This chapter is all about that. I've handpicked 10 plants with easy maintenance and stress-free. They won't die on you easily, so let's have a look!

1. SILVER POTHOS (*SCINDAPSUS PICTUS*)

The Silver Pothos is one of the easiest plants to look after and grow. It belongs to the Arum family, and it's an evergreen tropical vine. Unless you have very cold weather where you live, this plant is extremely beginner-friendly.

General Care

✿ **Light**

Bright, indirect light.

✿ **Soil**

Nutritious indoor potting mix with a combination of perlite, peat moss, and pine bark for optimal drainage.

✿ **Watering**

The plant doesn't do well in moist and soggy soil, so err on the side of less frequent watering. As always, poke your finger into the soil and if it feels dry, slowly pour some room-temperature water until it starts to seep out from the drainage holes at the bottom.

❀ **Temperature**

65 to 85 degrees Fahrenheit.

❀ **Humidity**

40% to 50%.

❀ **Fertilizer**

Feed once a month during summer and spring with a water-soluble houseplant fertilizer.

Potting and Repotting

You should repot your Silver Pothos if there's visible root growth under the pot through its drain holes. You might get to this point every one or two years depending on the rate of your plant's growth.

The best time to carry it out is right at the beginning of the growing season. Repot your Silver Pothos in a pot that's at least a couple of inches larger than your current one, and use a nutritious potting mix with excellent drainage (as mentioned above).

Propagation

Propagating this plant is also pretty straightforward! Simply snip some healthy cuttings about four inches from the top, and place them into a similar-sized pot with a suitable soil mix. Keep it in indirect light and let the soil remain moist until the plant roots. It should take about a month! Once it roots, you can start to slowly reduce your watering frequency.

2. PONYTAIL PALM (*BEAUCARNEA RECURVATA*)

Here's another viciously survivable plant – the Ponytail palm! Unless you overwater this plant, it'll stick with you through thick and thin. With long leafy streamers growing tall and arching out in all four directions – the plant's name seems pretty accurate! In their natural conditions, these plants can get as tall as 30 feet, but stay manageably short indoors at just 4 feet.

How to Grow

As an indoor plant, it's a "set and forget" type of grower as long as you provide it with sufficient light and a somewhat regular watering cycle. It doesn't grow fast though, so don't beat yourself over it if you don't see any additional foliage at the end of spring. It takes about two growing seasons for the plant to grow into a complete spectacle in your home collection.

General Care

✿ Light

Bright indirect light or full sun.

✿ Soil

Organically rich, sandy soil, or indoor succulent mix.

✿ Water

Once every one or two weeks (and skip it if it rains during that period).

✿ Temperature

Above 60 degrees Fahrenheit.

✿ Fertilizer

Slow-release pellet or liquid fertilizer in the growing season.

✿ Potting & Repotting

Repot into a small container with succulent potting mix every two to three years in the spring.

Propagating

Ponytail palms can grow pups that emerge as offsets from the base. You can remove and pot these individually to propagate a new ponytail plant out of them. A rooting hormone can also help stimulate new root growth in the pup to make up for the natural lack of roots on some offsets.

Pruning

Every once in a while, trim off damaged leaf sections whenever you spot them. You can also maintain a tidier appearance by pruning away any secondary shoots coming from the offsets from the plant's base – but that's optional, as some growers prefer the look of these secondary shoots.

3. MOTH ORCHID (PHALAENOPSIS ORCHID)

If you want a houseplant that's hard to kill, but doesn't look like it – the moth orchid is the perfect choice! Its delicate looks will almost scare you off as a novice, but it's actually pretty easy to maintain and grow (unless you plan on growing it outdoors in North America).

Growing Indoors

Being a tropical plant originating from the tropical parts of Asia and Australia, it's not cold-tolerant. But if you can maintain the right temperature for it, every-thing else is pretty straightforward. Here are the plant's preferred conditions for growing indoors:

✿ Light

Indirect daylight or artificial light.

✿ Temperature

75 to 85 degrees Fahrenheit.

✿ Humidity

50% to 80%.

✿ Watering

The plant has low drought tolerance, so you'll have to water it at least once a week. Slowly water it with warm or room-temperature water, and let it drain the excess out before repositioning it at its spot.

✿ Potting Soil

Moth orchid's root needs plenty of airflow, so make sure that the soil has good aeration and doesn't suffocate it. Also, ensure fresh airflow around the plant for optimal health and growth.

✿ Fertilizer

Use diluted orchid fertilizer every three or four weeks in the growing season.

Pruning

Once mature, orchids should be pruned once a year outside of the flowering period to get rid of faded blooms. Get some sterile scissors, and snip the stem's top portion to about an inch up from a node. This encourages more blooms and a new stem section. While you're at it, get rid of any brown/black leaves and snip away dead or mushy roots.

Potting and Repotting

You can repot moth orchids near the end of spring once they've already bloomed. But mature orchids can go about two to three years without a need for repotting, so you don't *have* to do it unless you see roots growing out of the drainage holes.

To report your Phalaenopsis, start by choosing a pot that's an inch or two larger than the previous one. Use a weak bleach solution to disinfect it, and then rinse and dry the container. Then, wash your hands and make sure that the tools you're about to use are sterile. Remove the orchid, cut away brown roots, and gently place it in the new one. It's recommended to use moistened bark as your potting medium and mist daily until you see new roots developing.

4. CHRISTMAS CACTUS (SCHLUMBERGERA)

The Christmas Cactus – also referred to as the "Holiday Cactus" – makes for the perfect gift in the festive season. That's because even if the person at the receiving end doesn't know much about plant maintenance, they'll still manage to look after this plant with ease with some basic care. The plant is flush with bold blooms that aren't even too picky about conditions!

General Care

✿ Light

Part-shade or diffused light.

✿ Soil

It's a highly adaptable plant that thrives in everything from a sandy, perlite, or loamy mix, to a standard cactus soil or a general purpose potting medium.

✿ Watering

Despite being a cactus, the plant is relatively thirstier due to its tropical origin. Water it thoroughly, let it drain out, and don't re-water until the soil is completely dry. In hot summers, this can be as quick as 2 days.

❀ Temperature

70 to 80 degrees Fahrenheit in growing months, and 55 to 65 degrees Fahrenheit otherwise.

❀ Humidity

50% to 60%.

❀ Fertilizer

Use a balanced, water-soluble, diluted half-strength fertilizer once a month during spring and summer.

❀ Pruning

Prune off the last one or two segments of the plant every year right after it blooms to make the plant branch out and grow more stems.

5. UMBRELLA TREE (SCHEFFLERA ARBORICOLA)

The large genus of tropical plants – the umbrella tree – has two particular species that stand out as ideal picks for indoor plant hobbyists. "Schefflera" is more of an umbrella term (pun-intended) that includes the Schefflera arboricola, and the Schefflera Actinophylla. They're both low-maintenance, prefer similar conditions, and add lots of aesthetic value to your space.

General Care

✿ Light

Indirect, bright light.

✿ Soil

Rich and somewhat moist.

✿ Watering

Water regularly (more so in its growth season), and let the soil dry out before each watering. You can slightly cut back on it during the winter months as continuously overwatering can kill the plant eventually.

✿ Temperature

60 to 75 degrees Fahrenheit.

✿ Humidity

75% and above.

✿ Fertilizer

Feed the plant once or (preferably) twice a week in spring with slow-release pellets or liquid fertilizer.

Pruning

Your umbrella plants may need some occasional pruning, especially if they somewhat lack daylight. Snip off anything that seems a bit leggy, overgrown, or brown. This plant responds well to pruning and rebounds with fuller growth.

6. CAST IRON PLANT (*ASPIDISTRA ELATIOR*)

The Cast Iron plant is notorious for being one of the most resilient houseplants out there. It's hard to kill even for the most negligent of plant parents. It has lance-shaped, glossy deep green leaves that grow about 2 feet in length and 4 inches wide. In other words, it's a stunning-looking plant!

General Care

✿ Light

A north-facing window is ideal as it keeps the plant safe from direct sunlight. The plant prefers a shady area with indirect sunlight.

✿ Soil

The plant isn't picky about its soil, being able to tolerate almost any soil type with decent drainage. A standard quality potting mix works great.

✿ Watering

The plant has some drought tolerance, adding to its "tough-to-kill" character. Only water the plant when you don't feel any dampness in the soil upon sticking your finger inside.

✿ Temperature

60 to 75 degrees Fahrenheit.

✿ Humidity

Prefers high humidity, but anything above 40% is a safe range.

✿ Fertilizer

Use all-purpose liquid fertilizer during the summer and spring months, following the instructions on the label.

Propagation

The most popular way to propagate cast-iron plants is by way of division (steps discussed earlier). It can be a costly plant in some parts of the world, so it's a pretty cheap and low-effort way to acquire a new plant for your home collection. Since it's such a survivable plant, it also makes for a great gift for your loved ones.

7. HINDU ROPE PLANT *(HOYA CARNOSA)*

The Hindu Rope plant is native to the East Asian and Australian regions and is commonly grown as an indoor plant in North America. It's classified as a semisucculent, vine-like, perennial species that is identifiable by its unique curling vines, lush and waxy foliage, and gorgeous blooms. It's also pretty low-maintenance!

General Care

❀ **Light**

Indirect, bright light (for maximum growth and bloom).

❀ **Soil**

Avoid using heavy soil for this plant. Instead, use a fast-draining, airy, and light potting mix. So, look for components like orchid bark or perlite.

❀ **Watering**

Being semi-succulents, they can naturally retain some water, allowing you to get away with infrequent watering. Only water the plant when the top inch or two are dried out, which can happen quickly during active growth season.

❀ **Temperature**

60 to 70 degrees Fahrenheit. Temperatures below 50 degrees Fahrenheit are not sustainable for this plant's growth and well-being.

❀ **Humidity**

40% to 60%.

✿ Fertilizer

The plant doesn't require any feed during the winter months. But using a weak fertilizer solution once every two months is sufficient during the rest of the year.

Propagating

You can easily propagate your Hindu Rope plant by way of replanting its stem cuttings, following the steps mentioned in earlier chapters. Just make sure to use light, airy, and well-drained potting soil – or plant your cuttings in water until roots develop.

How to Grow Hoya Carnosa From Seed

It's not easy to grow this plant from seed, and that's a well-known fact among houseplant hobbyists. Even if it works, it won't necessarily look anything like the original plant (yes, this one's weird). Your best bet is to propagate a cutting from your existing plant or buy a healthy plant from your nearest nursery.

8. PURPLE SHAMROCK *(FALSE SHAMROCK)*

The Purple Shamrock (or False Shamrock) is a pretty uncommon plant, but that's also what adds to its exotic vibe! Its black foliage sits well with that image, but it's actually an extremely deep purple shade if you look closely. Another unique element about their looks is their triangle leaves. It's easily one of the best-looking plants on this list (if not this whole book) – but that's subjective, of course.

Despite their delicate and outlandish appearance, the plant is actually pretty easy to look after.

General Care

❁ **Light**

Grows well in partial shade to full sun. About four hours of direct sun per day is ideal.

❁ **Soil**

A sandy or loamy soil works best as it naturally drains well.

❁ **Water**

Once mature, the plant is somewhat drought tolerant, though younger purple shamrock needs regular watering. During the growing season, water the plant when the top inch feels dry to the touch.

❁ **Temperature**

60 to 70 degrees Fahrenheit.

❁ **Humidity**

Around 50%.

✿ Fertilizer

During the growth season, use liquid or slow-release fertilizer according to the instructions on the label.

Propagation

The Purple Shamrock can be propagated by way of division (following the steps mentioned in earlier chapters). These plants can also be relatively expensive, so getting a new baby shamrock by way of division makes a lot of sense!

9. KAFFIR LILY (*CLIVIA MINIATA*)

The Kaffir Lily – also known as the Clivia plant – is almost invincible. They have blooms in distinctive color shades of orange, cream, and bright yellow – with trumpet-shaped flowers. Having one of these adorning your interior is going to be a huge talking point, especially during bloom season!

Blooming

Speaking of blooming, remember that the plant won't reward you with these gorgeous plants anytime soon! It takes about 2-3 years for this plant to grow old enough to bloom – and it mainly happens at the peak of spring season with some sporadic growth at its end.

General Care

As long as you get the basic conditions right (as listed below), the Kaffir Lily isn't a challenging plant to grow and maintain. At its peak, the plant stands about 18 inches tall and wide – but it'll take them about 2 to 5 years to get to that point.

✿ Light

Bright, indirect sunlight (but can live without much of it as well).

✿ Temperature

60 to 75 degrees Fahrenheit.

✿ Humidity

Prefers lower humidity (but can survive in the average home ambiance as well).

✿ Watering

Water your Kaffir Lily to keep the soil moist almost all the time during summer. In the winter, do it sparingly and let the soil dry out between waterings to encourage earlier blooms.

✿ Soil

Any well-drained potting mix that's high in organic matter.

✿ Repotting

The plant prefers being pot-bound, so only repot if necessary (but not during its flowering period).

Propagating

The two most common methods of propagating a Kaffir Lily is through division or seeds (both covered in earlier sections). Only propagate the plant once the spring season is over, as any additional stress during or before it can impact its bloom.

10. PARLOR PALM (*CHAMAEDOREA ELEGANS*)

The Parlor Palm takes up the last spot on this list, and it deserves it! It's naturally so survivable that if you cut a snipping of its fronds, it can survive for as long as six weeks despite being cut and detached from the plant! This also makes it a popular choice in flower arrangements for weddings and Palm Sunday decorations.

Growing it as an indoor palm is actually pretty common among houseplant enthusiasts thanks to its striking looks and low-maintenance nature.

General Care

✿ Light

Indirect, bright daylight.

✿ Soil

Can be planted in your yard outdoors, in some peaty soil as an indoor plant, or in any well-drained potting mix.

✿ Watering

Only water your Parlor Palm when the top inch of the soil feels completely dry to the touch. The plant is relatively sensitive to overwatering, so err on the side of dryness.

✿ Temperature

65 to 80 degrees Fahrenheit.

✿ Humidity

The plant cannot tolerate frost or cold drafts but thrives in average humidity.

✿ Fertilizer

This plant doesn't need much feeding. Some weak liquid fertilizer in the growing season (once or twice) would do.

Propagating Parlor Palm

The Parlor Palm is propagated directly from the seed, but mostly by professional growers. The success rate on this for home growers is depressingly low, so you'd best

234 | MICHE FERRET

stick to buying a new plant if you're looking to expand your Parlor Palm collection at home.

Potting and Repotting

The Parlor Palm has relatively slow-growing and sensitive root systems, so repotting should be done with extreme care, and only if necessary. The plant maintains a manageable size so repotting it once in two (or even three) years is sufficient.

CONCLUSION

This chapter has listed and described the basics of some of the most survivable plants in the world of greens! As a beginner, it makes sense to look for plants that won't die from the slightest bit of carelessness or negligence. Thankfully, hard-to-kill plants don't necessarily have to be boring!

Whether you're into gorgeous-looking plants like the Purple Shamrock, or ones with breathtaking blooms like the Kaffir Lily – there's always an option that doesn't require any tough commitments for maintenance.

No matter which plant you pick on this list, you'll surely be able to keep it happy and healthy regardless of your level of experience. All they need is some love, some water, and some daylight!

Speaking of daylight… what if you don't even get much sun where you live? Does that mean a planting hobby isn't for you? Absolutely not! The following chapter covers 10 plants that are best suited for low light conditions.

11

PLANTS SUITED TO LOW LIGHT

"Plants don't have a brain because they are not going anywhere."

— *ROBERT SYLWESTER*

Not all parts of the world are as blessed as the tropical or southern parts of the world when it comes to sunlight! Some countries have gray and gloomy weather almost all year round. In some parts of the world, nights can last as long as 18 hours in certain months (like December in Oslo). But, should the locals give up on their houseplant hobbies? Of course not!

Even if you live in a relatively sun-rich part of the world, you might still miss out on direct sunlight due to high-rise buildings all around you, a lack of tall windows, or simply living in the basement. Sometimes, you've just got to make the best out of what you've got.

If you can relate to such scenarios, this chapter is for you! It lists 10 plants with exceptional low-light tolerance! They are;

- Lucky Bamboo
- Sago Palm
- Nerve Plant
- Dumb Cane
- King Begonia
- Baby Rubber Plant
- Staghorn Fern
- Swiss Cheese Plant
- Boston Fern

No matter where you live, you still see trees and greenery outdoors – right? That's because life always finds a way to thrive, and so do these plants!

Regardless of how little light you get inside your room or home, you can still grow plants indoors and reap their countless health and wellness benefits. Sure, you'll have slightly limited options to choose from, but we've gathered an impressive list of low-light plants to make sure you don't feel left out!

Let's look at each of these special plants in detail.

1. LUCKY BAMBOO (DRACAENA SANDERIANA)

The Lucky Bamboo plant originated from Africa and is now commonly found in businesses, offices, and homes all around the world. It's rumored to bring the bearer some good fortune, hence the name "Lucky Bamboo."

While the plant could always use some indirect light, it can still survive and thrive in partial and complete shade. It's the ideal companion for your work desk, whether or not it gets enough sunlight (if at all).

General Care

❁ **Light**

Prefers partial shade but also thrives in shady conditions.

❁ **Soil**

Well-drained soil or water.

❁ Watering

Use distilled or bottled water for your lucky bamboo and keep the soil moist. If growing in water, change your vase water at least once a week.

❁ Temperature

63 to 90 degrees Fahrenheit. Keep the plant away from any potential sources of cold or hot drafts (windows, AC units, refrigerators, etc).

❁ Humidity

Average ambient humidity is fine for lucky bamboo.

❁ Fertilizer

Use only one drop of a liquid fertilizer every month is sufficient.

2. SAGO PALM (CYCAS REVOLUTA)

Ever thought you could fit a palm tree inside your home? Well, you can – at least a cuter, miniature version. Say hello to the Sago Palm! The plant is native to warm areas of southern China and Japan, and they're commonly grown as houseplants in places with cooler climates. The plant is great at tolerating low-light conditions, which is why it deserves a second place on this list.

General Care

✿ Light

The Sago Palm could use lots of direct sunlight but also comfortably thrives in partially shady conditions as well.

✿ Soil

Well-draining sandy soil.

✿ Watering

The plant has decent drought tolerance, but prefers slightly moist soil. Feel free to top it off with some water whenever the soil feels a bit dry. Cut back on watering in the winter months.

✿ Temperature

65 to 75 degrees Fahrenheit.

✿ Fertilizer

Use an 18-8-18 ratio liquid fertilizer once a month from spring to fall – i.e. the plant's growing season.

✿ Pruning

Prune away leaves that have fully turned brown and leave the yellow ones intact.

3. NERVE PLANT

Nerve plants love their sunlight, but are highly adaptable and also handle low-light conditions well. This plant's most common variant is white, but it also comes in green, red, and pink varieties. Growing no taller than 3 to 6 inches, this plant is perfect for your desk – even if it gets little to no sunlight.

General Care

✿ Light

Part shade or filtered indirect sunlight.

✿ Soil

Well-drained, moist soil.

✿ Watering

The nerve plant has little to no drought resistance and can die from underwatering relatively easily. Make sure to keep the soil moist at all times and perform daily finger-poking tests on the soil to make sure that the top inch or two doesn't dry out.

✿ Temperature

Around 70 degrees Fahrenheit.

✿ Humidity

60% to 70%.

✿ Fertilizer

Feed your nerve plants weekly during the growing season with a 50% diluted dose of a 5-5-5 tropical plant liquid fertilizer.

Pruning

The nerve plant is a fast grower, especially when it gets exposed to the right conditions. Remember to check for leggy stems and regularly pinch off the tips to maintain full and bushy foliage growth.

Propagating

The simplest and most common way to propagate this plant is by replanting some healthy leaf cuttings. We've discussed this method in detail before so make sure to follow those steps carefully!

Pro Tip: Using a rooting hormone can encourage root growth and heighten your chances of success while propagating a nerve plant.

Potting and Repotting

You should repot your nerve plants annually during early summer or spring. Use a pot with large enough

244 | MICHE FERRET

drainage holes at the bottom, and fill it up with some conventional gardening potting mix. Replant your nerve plant gently into it and you're done!

4. DUMB CANE (DIEFFENBACHIA)

The Dieffenbachias have ovate, pointed leaves that come in white, cream, and green colors – depending on the variety you purchase. They're known to reach dimensions of 10 feet in height, and 20 inches in length. The plant prefers lots of filtered light for optimal growth of new, tender leaves, but the plant still thrives in partly shady conditions.

General Care

✿ Light

Indirect light or part shade.

✿ Soil

Well-drained potting soil, preferably with peat as one of the major components in the mix.

✿ Watering

The Dieffenbachias do not like dryness, especially in the peak season for growth. Make sure to regularly enrich their soil with moisture, with frequency as high as twice a week. Cut back watering during the winter months as the plant uses up less moisture out of its growing season, and the residual moisture dries out slower due to cold temperatures.

✿ Temperature

60 to 75 degrees Fahrenheit – with no exposure to cold drafts.

✿ Humidity

60%.

✿ Fertilizer

Feed the plant once every 4 to 6 weeks with a balanced 20-20-20 fertilizer with diluted strength.

5. KING BEGONIA (BEGONIA REX)

Low-light tolerant plants can look awesome, and the Begonia Rex is living proof of that! It's one of the most dramatic looking plants out there, having leaves with a deep shade of red as its most common form. The attractive shades of purple and maroon get even more vibrant as the plant is exposed to more bright light, but it still comfortably survives in low-light conditions.

General Care

✿ Light

Part shade to full shade.

✿ Soil

Porous soil mix that's light, airy, and well-drained.

✿ Watering

Regularly water your King Begonia plant, but be careful not to overwater it. Don't water it unless the surface of the soil is dry to the touch.

✿ Temperature

60 to 70 degrees Fahrenheit.

✿ Humidity

Around 50%.

✿ Fertilizer

Use a half- or quarter-strength liquid fertilizer on a fortnightly basis to ensure optimal nutrition for your King Begonia.

6. BABY RUBBER PLANT (*PEPEROMIA OBTUSIFOLIA*)

The Peperomia Obtusifolia – or the Baby Rubber Plant – is another great low-light tolerant indoor plant. It has South American origins, and is known for its upright, thick stems with round leaves. The glossy, vibrant green shade of leaves – paired with a unique shape – makes this plant a highly decorative element inside your home.

General Care

✿ Light

Prefers indirect light (medium to bright), but thrives in low light as well.

✿ Soil

Best soil is an aerated, well-drained soil with components like coconut coir, perlite, worm casting, activated charcoal, and orchid bark.

✿ Watering

Water once or twice a week, giving the potting mix enough time to dry out in between.

✿ Temperature

65 to 75 degrees Fahrenheit.

✿ Humidity

40% to 50%.

✿ Size

This plant stays manageably small indoors, especially in low-light conditions. It won't grow any taller than two feet, making it the perfect work desk companion.

7. STAGHORN FERN (*PLATYCERIUM*)

The Platycerium's foliage has a peculiar resemblance to the antlers of an elk or a deer, earning it the name "Staghorn." The plant is native to Australia and Asia. It grows relatively slowly, but doesn't stop until it's one of the largest indoor plants in your home collection!

As long as you provide the Staghorn Fern with sufficient humidity, it won't complain about the lack of daylight. Guess where this plant naturally fits inside your home? Yep – your shower!

General Care

✿ Light

Prefers partial shade.

✿ Soil

Being an epiphyte, the Staghorn Fern needs a starting lump of moss, compost, peat, and other organic matter – with no additional soil required.

✿ Watering

This plant demands frequent watering, but enough time in between for at least the base to dry out. This can take about a week in the summer months and up to three weeks in the winter.

✿ Temperature

80 to 90 degrees Fahrenheit, but thrives in anything over 60 degrees Fahrenheit.

✿ Humidity

70% to 80%. It's advisable to place these in your shower.

✿ Fertilizer

Feed the plant on a monthly basis with a water-soluble, balanced fertilizer.

8. SWISS CHEESE PLANT (MONSTERA)

The Swiss Cheese Plant – or "Monstera" – is native to the massive Central American rainforests. In its natural habitat, this plant grows to be bold and massive. Being a climbing evergreen that's super easy to grow, it's a pretty popular choice amongst houseplant enthusiasts. Its classy appearance can also add loads of visual appeal to any interior design plan, and the manageable growth rate of 1 to 2 feet a year also helps its viability as a domestic plant.

General Care

✿ Light

Prefers indirect bright sunlight, but also thrives in part shade.

✿ Soil

Well-drained, peat-based potting mix.

✿ Watering

The plant doesn't need too much water to thrive. In spring, water it once or twice on a fortnightly basis, giving it lots of time to dry out in between.

✿ Temperature

60 to 80 degrees Fahrenheit.

✿ Humidity

Anything above 40%.

✿ Fertilizer

Top the plant off with a 20-20-20 balanced fertilizer every 2-3 weeks during spring and summer.

Pruning

The Monstera Deliciosa needs occasional trimming to get rid of aerial roots. If you don't like snipping your plants unless necessary, you can also tuck these roots into the plant's pot.

9. BOSTON FERN (*NEPHROLEPIS EXALTATA*)

The Boston Fern is cheap, awesome-looking, and not-so-needy when it comes to lighting needs. Hang a few of these in a basket and they'll make any interior look ten times better! The plant is also known as "Sword Fern" and is a pretty popular species of fern, naturally occurring in tropical regions globally. It's commonly grown as a houseplant in North America since it doesn't need much light and is relatively easy to maintain.

General Care

✿ Light

Prefers lots of indirect bright light, but thrives in shady conditions as well.

❀ Soil and Drainage

Boston Fern requires a loamy, well-drained soil that's high in organic matter. Adding components like peat, compost, and perlite make the ideal potting mix for this plant.

❀ Watering

Always keep this plant's soil slightly moist, but be careful not to overwater it. You'll probably have to water it once a week, or more frequently in warmer conditions.

❀ Temperature

65 to 75 degrees Fahrenheit.

❀ Humidity

Anything above 50%.

❀ Fertilizer

Doesn't require much feed. Feed indoor ferns with a liquid houseplant fertilizer having a 20-10-20 composition in summer and spring, with no added fertilizers during fall and winter.

CONCLUSION

That sums up our selection of some of the best low-light tolerant houseplants out there. This, by no means, is an exhaustive list! There are many more gorgeous and highly beneficial houseplants out there that can thrive (and even prefer) shady conditions. However, the plants discussed in this chapter were chosen for a combination of their humble lighting needs, gorgeous appearance, and ease of maintenance.

So, even if you get little to no direct sunlight at home, you can still take part in the houseplant game without compromising any of the thrill, fun, and health benefits that come with it.

PARTING WORDS

If you've read this book all the way to this point, one thing's for sure – you know a whole lot more about houseplants than you did before. Starting from the basics like the building blocks of plant life – air, water, and light – to complex propagating procedures, you've learned it all! Hopefully, you now understand that it's actually simple to choose, pot, repot, and even propagate your own plants at home.

With so many health and wellness benefits of taking up this hobby, it's surprising (and sad) that a vast majority of people steer away from it. Most of them fear the daily commitment of looking after plants or killing them unintentionally, and many just don't have the time to give it a proper thought.

By now, you hopefully understand how there's a plant for every type of person out there, even for absolute beginners who can be forgetful, negligent, and completely inexperienced – and *still* get away with it.

So, now that YOU understand all the basics to confidently buy some houseplants and grow them indoors – it's time to take the first step. Who knows, you might be born with an incredible green thumb and don't even know it yet!

Feel free to start with hard-to-kill plants to ease into it, and slowly move up the ladder with more challenging plant projects. You might even inspire a few family members just by showing them how easy and rewarding it actually is!

Wish you all the best on this exciting journey of being a plant parent. Happy growing!

REFERENCES

21 pros and cons of natural pesticides vs. synthetic pesticides. Pest Control FAQ. (2020, August 19). Retrieved from https://pestcontrolfaq. com/natural-pesticides-vs-synthetic-pesticides/

Aglaonema care. Greenery Unlimited. (n.d.). Retrieved August 16, 2022, from https://greeneryunlimited.co/blogs/plant-care/aglaonema-care

Akin, C. (2022, March 25). *The top 10 secrets for becoming a houseplant whisperer.* Houseplant Resource Center. Retrieved from https:// houseplantresourcecenter.com/2020/06/the-top-10-secrets-for-becoming-a-houseplant-whisperer/

Beaulieu, D. (2021, August 31). *How to grow and care for purple shamrock (false shamrock).* The Spruce. Retrieved August 16, 2022, from https://www.thespruce.com/purple-shamrock-plants-2132875

Beck, A. (2022, May 31). *How to water houseplants the right way (and how to know if you're overwatering).* Better Homes & Gardens. Retrieved from https://www.bhg.com/gardening/houseplants/care/water ing-houseplants/

Beginners Plant Buying Guide: 10 tips for buying houseplants. Omysa. (2021, April 26). Retrieved from https://blog.omysa.com/plant-care/10-tips-for-buying-houseplants/

The best potting soil for indoor plants - complete guide. Smart Garden Guide. (2019, December 8). Retrieved from https://smartgarden guide.com/best-potting-soil-for-indoor-plants/

Damman, A. (2022, March 8). *The top 7 health benefits of Houseplants.* Seattle's Favorite Garden Store Since 1924 - Swansons Nursery. Retrieved August 16, 2022, from https://www.swansonsnursery. com/blog/health-benefits-of-houseplants

Damman, A. (2022, March 8). *The top 7 health benefits of Houseplants.* Seattle's Favorite Garden Store Since 1924 - Swansons Nursery.

Retrieved August 16, 2022, from https://www.swansonsnursery.com/blog/health-benefits-of-houseplants

Damman, A. (2022, March 9). *How to repot a plant*. Seattle's Favorite Garden Store Since 1924 - Swansons Nursery. Retrieved August 16, 2022, from https://www.swansonsnursery.com/blog/how-to-repot-a-plant

Dian. (2022, July 8). *7 homemade plant sprays for Your Outdoor Garden*. Dian Farmer Learning To Grow Our Own Food. Retrieved from https://dianfarmer.com/7-homemade-plant-sprays-for-your-outdoor-garden/

Farm, L. O. (2019, February 17). *Loch Organic Farm*. http://homestead brooklyn.com/all/2017/1... - Loch Organic Farm. Retrieved from https://www.facebook.com/LochOrganicFarm/posts/2167946903244129

Flaming Katy. Kalanchoe blossfeldiana Indoor Plant Care. (n.d.). Retrieved August 16, 2022, from https://www.guide-to-house plants.com/flaming-katy.html

Fresh, F. T. D. (2020, December 2). *20 popular types of succulents*. FTD.-com. Retrieved August 16, 2022, from https://www.ftd.com/blog/share/types-of-succulents

Garden, N. (2021, January 8). *Ficus care*. New Garden Landscaping & Nursery | Landscape, Design & Garden Centers. Retrieved August 16, 2022, from https://newgarden.com/learning-center/ficus-care

GARDENING, R. H. S. (2022, January 1). *Houseplants: To support human health / RHS gardening*. Retrieved August 16, 2022, from https://www.rhs.org.uk/plants/types/houseplants/for-human-health

General Indoor and outdoor bromeliad care. Bromeliad Plant Care. (2016, June 20). Retrieved August 16, 2022, from https://www.bromeliads.info/general-indoor-outdoor-bromeliad-care/

A guide to fungus and houseplants (what's harmful and what's not, and how to fix it). WallyGrow. (n.d.). Retrieved from https://wallygrow.com/blogs/feature/fungus-and-houseplants#:

Holmes, K. (2020, January 21). *Everything you need to know about ZZ plants*. Gardenista. Retrieved August 16, 2022, from https://www.

gardenista.com/posts/everything-you-need-to-know-about-zz-plants-zamioculcas-zamiifolia/

How do indoor plants affect people's mood? HortiBiz. (2021, November 9). Retrieved August 16, 2022, from https://www.hortibiz.com/newsitem/news/how-do-indoor-plants-affect-peoples-mood/

How to care for a devil's ivy. Greener House. (n.d.). Retrieved August 16, 2022, from https://www.greenerhousenursery.com/blogs/articles/devils-ivy-care-guide

Hughes, M. (2020, September 10). *4 tips for choosing the best containers for your houseplants.* Better Homes & Gardens. Retrieved from https://www.bhg.com/gardening/houseplants/care/choosing-houseplants/

Iannotti, M. (2022, June 2). *How to grow and care for Aloe Vera.* The Spruce. Retrieved August 16, 2022, from https://www.thespruce.com/grow-aloe-vera-1403153

Indoor Panda Plant: Tips for growing Kalanchoe Panda plants. (n.d.). Retrieved August 17, 2022, from https://www.gardeningknowhow.com/houseplants/kalanchoe/indoor-panda-plant-care.htm

Indoor Plants Lighting Guide. House Plant Lighting Guide - Indoor Plants Light Requirements. (n.d.). Retrieved from https://www.houseplantsexpert.com/indoor-plants-lighting-guide.html

Information on pincushion cactus care - gardening know how. (n.d.). Retrieved August 17, 2022, from https://www.gardeningknowhow.com/ornamental/cacti-succulents/pincushion-cactus/pincushion-cactus-care.htm

Jade Plant Care Instructions: How to care for a jade plant. (n.d.). Retrieved August 17, 2022, from https://www.gardeningknowhow.com/houseplants/jade-plant/jade-plant-care.htm

Johnson, E. (2021, July 21). *How to grow and care for Haworthia Plants.* Apartment Therapy. Retrieved August 16, 2022, from https://www.apartmenttherapy.com/how-to-grow-and-care-for-haworthia-plants-36638507

Layering propagation for the home gardener - Oklahoma State University. Layering Propagation for the Home Gardener | Oklahoma State University. (2017, February 1). Retrieved August 16, 2022, from https://extension.okstate.edu/fact-sheets/layering-propagation-for-the-home-gardener.html

Marie Claire 10/06/2020 11:20 am. (2021, April 8). *Houseplants are the ultimate stress relievers for your home.* Marie Claire. Retrieved from https://www.marieclaire.co.uk/life/health-fitness/houseplants-stress-reliever-stress-month-653559

MasterClass. (2021, March 18). *Crown of Thorns Plant Care: How To Grow Crown of thorns - 2022.* MasterClass. Retrieved August 16, 2022, from https://www.masterclass.com/articles/crown-of-thorns-plant-guide#what-is-a-crown-of-thorns-plant

MasterClass. (2021, March 25). *Panda Plant Care Guide: How To Grow kalanchoe tomentosa - 2022.* MasterClass. Retrieved August 16, 2022, from https://www.masterclass.com/articles/panda-plant-care-guide

Miracle-Gro 72 68. (2022, August 16). *How to grow jade plants.* Miracle. Retrieved August 16, 2022, from https://www.miraclegro.com/en-us/library/indoor-gardening/how-grow-jade-plants

Panda Plant Care Guide: How To Grow kalanchoe tomentosa - 2022. MasterClass. (n.d.). Retrieved August 16, 2022, from https://www.masterclass.com/articles/panda-plant-care-guide

Philodendron Care Guide: How To Grow philodendron plants - 2022. MasterClass. (n.d.). Retrieved August 16, 2022, from https://www.masterclass.com/articles/philodendron-care

Plantas, C. (n.d.). *Oxalis corniculata or creeping woodsorrel: Care and growing.* BACK TO TOP. Retrieved August 16, 2022, from http://www.consultaplantas.com/index.php/en/plants-from-m-to-r/2496-oxalis-corniculata-or-creeping-woodsorrel-care-and-growing

Prestigious. (2022, March 4). *How plants reduce fatigue & improve employee productivity.* Prestigious Plantscapes. Retrieved from https://www.prestigiousplantscapes.com.au/reduce-worker-fatigue-with-indoor-plants/

Propagation tips. Lush Little Jungle. (n.d.). Retrieved August 16, 2022, from https://lushlittlejungle.com/pages/propagation-tips

Sansevieria 101: How to care for snake plants. Bloomscape. (2022,

February 1). Retrieved August 16, 2022, from https://bloomscape. com/plant-care-guide/sansevieria/

Karen. (2022, May 3). *Roseum plant 'Sedum Spurium' - the perfect addition to your garden.* Succulent City. Retrieved August 17, 2022, from https://succulentcity.com/sedum-spurium-roseum-plant/

Seven methods of plant propagation. Plant Cell Technology | Your partner in plant tissue culture. (2020, November 12). Retrieved from https://www.plantcelltechnology.com/blog/seven-methods-of-plant-propagation/

The Sill. (2018, May 2). *Water Plant Propagation for Beginners.* The Sill. Retrieved from https://www.thesill.com/blogs/diy/plant-propaga tion-for-beginners

The Sill. (2019, August 7). *How to care for the Haworthia succulent: Plants 101.* The Sill. Retrieved August 16, 2022, from https://www.thesill. com/blogs/plants-101/how-to-care-for-haworthia

The Sill. (2019, September 6). *How to care for oxalis: Plant care articles & how-tos.* The Sill. Retrieved August 16, 2022, from https://www. thesill.com/blogs/plants-101/how-to-care-for-oxalis-oxalis-spp

Succulen. (2018, April 4). *7 benefits of growing succulents in your home.* Succulents. Retrieved August 16, 2022, from https://www.succu lents.net/7-benefits-growing-succulents-home/

Tips & information about burro's tail - gardening know how. (n.d.). Retrieved August 16, 2022, from https://www.gardeningknowhow. com/ornamental/cacti-succulents/burros-tail

VanZile, J. (2022, April 12). *How to grow & care for schefflera (umbrella plant).* The Spruce. Retrieved August 16, 2022, from https://www. thespruce.com/grow-schefflera-plants-inside-1902771

VanZile, J. (2022, August 3). *Dieffenbachia (Dumb Cane): Plant Care & Growing Guide.* The Spruce. Retrieved August 16, 2022, from https://www.thespruce.com/dumb-cane-dieffenbachia-definition-1902751

VanZile, J. (2022, July 16). *How to grow and shape lucky bamboo.* The Spruce. Retrieved August 16, 2022, from https://www.thespruce. com/growing-lucky-bamboo-1902994

VanZile, J. (2022, June 24). *A handy guide to the snake plant (dracaena trifasciata)*. The Spruce. Retrieved August 16, 2022, from https://www.thespruce.com/snake-plant-care-overview-1902772

VanZile, J. (2022, June 24). *Dracaena plant (Dragon Tree): A perfect house-plant for beginners*. The Spruce. Retrieved August 16, 2022, from https://www.thespruce.com/grow-dracaena-marginata-indoors-1902749

Williams, M. (2020, June 6). *How to grow burro's tail, a delicate but beautiful succulent*. Apartment Therapy. Retrieved August 16, 2022, from https://www.apartmenttherapy.com/burros-tail-plant-care-36756368

Made in United States
Troutdale, OR
11/16/2023